Robin Gill is Michael Ramsey Pro
at the University of Kent and Hoi
Canterbury Cathedral. He has writte
A Bit Like Jesus and many other bo
applied theology, including *A Textbook of Christian Ethics* (third
edition 2006) and *Health Care and Christian Ethics* (2006). For
13 years he chaired the Archbishop of Canterbury's Medical Ethics
Advisory Group and he is currently a member of the Nuffield
Council on Bioethics and the British Medical Association's
committee on medical ethics (although he writes here purely
on his own behalf and not to represent any of these bodies). At
parish level he leads a clergy team serving five rural congregations
in Kent.

NEW CHALLENGES
FOR CHRISTIANS

From test-tube babies to euthanasia

Robin Gill

First published in Great Britain in 2010

Society for Promoting Christian Knowledge
36 Causton Street
London SW1P 4ST
www.spckpublishing.co.uk

British Library Cataloguing-in-Publication Data
A catalogue record for this book is available from the British Library

ISBN 978–0–281–06280–5

1 3 5 7 9 10 8 6 4 2

Typeset by Graphicraft Ltd, Hong Kong
Printed in Great Britain by Ashford Colour Press

Produced on paper from sustainable forests

Contents

———•◆•———

Contents

Part 3
ABORTION AND FERTILITY TREATMENT

Part 4
DOCTORS AND PATIENTS

Part 5
SEXUALITY AND FAMILIES

Part 6
ASSISTED DYING

Preface

My SPCK Lent book *A Bit Like Jesus* (2009) looked at the healing stories and parables of Jesus within the Gospels, suggesting that they offer important values – compassion, care, faith and humility – that can still shape our lives today. *New Challenges for Christians* seeks to complement that book. Addressing the same wide audience, it takes these values and applies them to emerging ethical dilemmas in the complex worlds of genetics, healthcare and sexuality today.

Much of my working life as an applied theologian is spent among secular colleagues both at the University of Kent and in various medical ethics committees in London. Often I am the only theologian present. Occasionally I tease those who are militantly secular, trying to persuade them to disaggregate the two words 'blind' and 'faith' or to attempt sentences that do not unstintingly contain 'religious' and 'dogma' together. In even naughtier moments I point to the empirical evidence suggesting that churchgoing may actually be good for one's health. But most of the time I simply enjoy their company and learn from them enormously. Applied theologians work among secular colleagues but try not to appear too holy to be relevant and live among the religiously minded but try not to be too faithless.

Writing articles for a wider public has been one of the ways that I have tried to mediate what I have learned from secular colleagues back to discerning churchgoers. Applied theologians, especially, have a duty to communicate not just with their fellow academic theologians but also with a wider body of churchpeople, as well as with members of the general public. It is our job to try to relate faith and practice and to do so as professionally and as clearly as possible. Doing a short piece for a church or secular newspaper on a complex and emerging ethical issue can be a risky business. Sometimes it evokes quite tart and even intemperate responses. Yet it is a good means of testing professionalism and clarity.

Quite a number of the shorter pieces that follow were written specifically for *Church Times*. But their titles were usually changed and some of the contents reduced to save space. However, they are reproduced here (with permission) more as they were originally written, albeit with notes to bring them up to date or to indicate where a more academic discussion can be found. Longer pieces either appear here in print for the first time or were published in a collection or journal as indicated again in a note.

The date when first written has deliberately been given for each piece. Sharp-eyed readers may soon spot some shifts in my own responses over time. For example, earlier pieces on assisted fertility leave open the possibility that genetic engineering might one day be used ethically to eliminate egregious single-gene defects. In contrast, later pieces suggest that the introduction of the new technique of pre-implantation genetic diagnosis (PGD) could be a much safer, and thus more ethical, means of achieving this. Or again, earlier pieces in the area of assisted dying distinguish withdrawing or withholding life-sustaining treatment from involuntary euthanasia on the basis that the latter involves an 'intention' to end life. Yet the later pieces by-pass 'intention' and treat 'euthanasia' in a much broader way. The reason for this change is that subsequent legal analysis of the crucial Law Lords judgment in 1992 has raised the possibility that the judges involved really did 'intend' to allow the ending of lives of patients who were permanently insensate and comatose (so-called PVS patients).

All of this is still highly disputed territory. And these are very much articles in progress. However, I do hope that you enjoy them even if you disagree with their (ever fallible) conclusions.

Part 1
GROUNDINGS

Churchgoing and moral attitudes

1996

Does churchgoing shape people's moral attitudes and behaviour? Until recently sociologists, and indeed many theologians, have tended to be sceptical. There is long-standing evidence that churchgoers tend to be more orthodox in their religious beliefs than non-churchgoers – although even here belief is by no means confined to churchgoers or disbelief to non-churchgoers. But it has been more difficult to find convincing evidence that churchgoing has much effect upon moral attitudes, let alone upon moral behaviour.

Is this because the evidence does not exist, or is it rather that scholars have never looked properly for it? At last we have some convincing evidence that it is the latter. For the first time the annual British Social Attitudes (BSA) survey presents strong evidence for the significance of churchgoing in three separate moral areas.

Many newspapers reported the general findings from the latest report of BSA.[1] They particularly noticed perceptions of greater inequality as well as a surprising resilience in family relationships despite growing divorce. What they largely failed to notice is that in this family area, as well as in attitudes towards euthanasia and towards sex and swearing in films and on television, churchgoers differ significantly from non-churchgoers. In fact, in each area there is a clear process – measured by the statistical process of regression analysis – showing that the more frequently individuals go to church, the more likely they are to hold 'traditional' moral values.

Each year BSA – described by *The Times* as the Rolls-Royce of surveys – have asked people about their religious affiliation and about whether and how often they go to a place of worship, along-side a host of other questions on politics, health, culture, leisure and moral attitudes. Yet they have seldom analysed religion as a moral variable. They have usually assumed that it is factors such as gender, age and social class which are the important variables, even on moral issues. The 1984 and 1987 surveys were exceptions. Analysing data on personal honesty, they noted that churchgoers did appear to be different from others. For instance, they found that whereas only 9 per cent of weekly churchgoers thought it was not really wrong for a householder to overclaim on insurance for flood damage to make £500, this rose to 12 per cent for monthly attenders, to 18 per cent for infrequent attenders, to 22 per cent for non-attenders and to 24 per cent for those claiming no religion. Another ten honesty questions between the two surveys found a comparable trend. Some of these questions asked for a general moral judgment and others for a specific judgment about what those being asked might do in such a situation. Overall, churchgoers appeared significantly more honest than non-churchgoers.

Nevertheless, these earlier reports maintained that it was only in matters of personal morality that churchgoers were distinct. On social issues differences between churchgoers and others could be accounted for by age (with the exception of Roman Catholics on abortion). They assumed that churchgoers, on average more elderly than the general population, simply reflected the social values of an older generation.

I was puzzled by this claim since it was made without much supporting evidence. As I already had indications from other (largely ignored) surveys that churchgoing may shape moral attitudes beyond the purely personal, I decided to investigate the issue more directly. So six months ago I set up a research project examining previous data from the BSA surveys, specifically testing whether or not churchgoing affects morality. The project still continues but it has already shown that the moral distinctiveness of churchgoers has been seriously underestimated by many scholars. In at least ten different moral areas – including attitudes towards work, unjust laws, racism, environmental concern and action, charitable giving, and involvement in voluntary work in the community – churchgoing is a very good predictor of behaviour.[2]

The new BSA survey appears to confirm this, showing a very rough comparison of trends. All reflect mean scores: a series of responses are combined to give a scale between permissive and traditional attitudes (the report uses the terms 'libertarian' and 'authoritarian' which, of course, gives a rather different slant). So the family-orientation scale combines responses to such statements as 'People should keep in touch with close family members even if they don't have much in common' and the contrasting 'On the whole, my friends are more important to me than members of my family.' The euthanasia scale is particularly sophisticated, combining pro- or anti-euthanasia responses on eight very different cases – ranging from a permanent vegetative state (PVS) patient to someone without a terminal illness who was simply tired of life.

Two observations about this evidence. First, there is a great deal of overlap between churchgoers and non-churchgoers. These are not isolated groups. For example, in analysing a 1994 question about whether people thought that the right to show nudity and sex in films and magazines had gone too far, I found that 88 per cent of churchgoers thought that it had. Nonetheless, 63 per cent of non-churchgoers and 50 per cent of those claiming no religion also had the same view. And there was one middle-aged weekly churchgoer who thought that it had not gone far enough (there always is one!).

Second, *on average* churchgoers are distinct from non-churchgoers and they are distinct across age groups. Again on the question about nudity, at least 85 per cent of weekly attenders in all age groups thought that it had gone too far. There were very significant generational differences in the no-religion group: in the oldest group 90 per cent objected to media nudity, whereas in the youngest group it was only 38 per cent. Nonetheless, age was not the only factor involved – churchgoing was also clearly significant.

But is it really churchgoing which shapes morality? It might simply be that people with traditional moral attitudes are more likely to go to church. There may be some truth in this, yet there are also indications that it is not the whole of the truth. For example, the fact that the youngest generation of churchgoers shows distinct moral views counts against it. Presumably this is a group which has largely been socialized to be churchgoers, differing from, say, parents who decide to start going to church in order to encourage their children to have a sense of morality. Again, the evidence from surveys such as John Finney's 1992 *Finding Faith Today*, as well as Mass Observation research reported in the January 1949 *British Weekly*, suggests that most people go back to church as a result of having Christian friends, partners or spouses. Conversely, they stop going to church because they move house, lose interest or change lifestyle, rather than because they change their religious or moral beliefs. Beliefs may be retained by lapsed churchgoers for many years (what Grace Davie terms 'believing without belonging'[3]), although they may not be passed on so readily to their children.

Only in-depth qualitative research (which I hope to do later) can finally unravel the complex relationship between churchgoing and moral attitudes and behaviour. Yet the British Social Attitudes data is already proving more interesting than many might have supposed. Perhaps it really is the contents of worship – singing hymns of faith, listening to the Bible, engaging in intercessory prayer and even hearing regular sermons – that may after all shape our moral visions.

Is Christian ethics distinctive?

1999

Bishop Richard Holloway's views on sex and drugs are characteristically robust. Over the last week they have provoked considerable controversy. However, at the heart of his new book *Godless Morality*[1] is a serious and important issue which still concerns and divides scholars in Christian ethics. Is it possible to express what is distinctive about Christian ethics without denying the validity of other forms of ethics? Does Christian ethics inevitably clash with secular ethics and perhaps also with ethics drawn from other religious traditions? Or can Christian ethicists successfully work alongside other ethicists, both with those from other religious traditions and with those disavowing any religious tradition at all?

Richard Holloway puts his own stance pithily in his subtitle, *Keeping Religion out of Ethics*. Baroness Warnock, who carefully separates her own influential writings on ethics from her more private Christian faith, commends the book warmly on its cover. In contrast, his colleague Dr Kevin Scott argues this week in *The Scotsman* that

> at bottom, Richard Holloway seems to believe that the Church has nothing to offer and if it does offer something, it does so with an ulterior motive of seeking to bring people under its power ... But in his dismissal of Christian moral authority, in the deconstruction of the ministry of his own parish priests, he deconstructs his own episcopacy.[2]

Can Richard Holloway's position really be sustained in Christian ethics? The radical Dominican scholar Herbert McCabe has argued for something very like it on the basis of his understanding of natural law. For example, it could be argued that moral reasoning is common to all people regardless of their religious faith. The latter is to do with salvation, not morality. However, such a neat division is quite difficult to sustain in practice and classical theologians such as Thomas Aquinas saw clear continuities between natural law and revelation. The primary Christian virtues of faith, hope and love do seem to have both moral and religious implications.

A contrasting position, which has become popular in much Christian ethics today, holds that it is only within communities of faith that we can acquire moral virtues at all. The US Christian ethicist Stanley Hauerwas has been immensely influential over the last two decades.[3] Hauerwas argues that Christian ethics should be primarily concerned with Christian character within worshipping communities. As the world at large becomes increasingly estranged from these communities, so Christians rapidly become 'resident aliens'. As a result, we must renounce the Enlightenment and challenge secular society with our Christian faith and with the values derived directly from it. Conversion, not co-operation, is now required.

A third position argues that if Christians can work with others without denying our own faith then we should always attempt to do so. This position has been especially important among those of us working in medical ethics. In all Western countries today Christian doctors and nurses work alongside those with other religious faiths and with none, and patients, in turn, will probably not know whether those treating them share their own faith or not. Of course, there may be areas where there is a considerable conflict – as traditionalist Roman Catholics have found on reproductive issues and Jehovah's Witnesses have found on blood transfusions. Yet it is overwhelmingly in the interests of most of us, Christians and non-Christians alike, that current medical practice should not conflict with our own values.

Unlike the Holloway approach, this last position argues that Christian ethics differs most from secular ethics at the level of underlying justification. Christians do have distinctive resources – the Bible, Christian tradition and experience in Christian worship – which provide underlying justification for our ethics and moral behaviour. Yet Christians do not necessarily agree with each other on specific moral issues (such as abortion). And unlike the Hauerwas approach, this third position holds that Christian communities overlap at many points with secular communities, from which we can learn as well as seeking to influence them. Faithful co-operation, rather than separation or confrontation, is the hallmark of this final position.

Changing attitudes

1999

The 1998 survey findings of BSA have now been published and, among many other issues, show important changes in attitudes to religion and morality over the last 15 years. BSA is widely used by government and university departments, but seldom by churches. This is a pity because it offers some important clues about trends, free from the sort of spin that now characterizes statistics produced by churches themselves.

Two of the most dramatic changes arise from the question, 'Do you regard yourself as belonging to any particular religion?' In 1983, 31 per cent said they had no religion and 40 per cent said that they were Anglican. In 1998 it is now 45 per cent who claim no religion and only 27 per cent who claim to be Anglican. These two striking trends have been plotted by all of the BSA surveys over the last 15 years and do seem to be firmly established. People in Britain today, especially the young, are less inclined than before to claim nominal church membership, opting instead for no religion.

As expected, overall levels of claimed churchgoing across denominations have declined during this same period, but this decline is not nearly as striking as the two other trends. In 1983, 21 per cent of those interviewed claimed to go to church at least once a month, but by 1998 this had dropped to 19 per cent. The drop has been particularly among those claiming to go every week, without a corresponding increase in monthly churchgoers. Despite claims to the contrary, it does seem that somewhat fewer people go to church, not that the same number of people go to church but less often.

A slight health warning is needed here: a gap between stated and actual behaviour has long been noted by sociologists. On the basis of BSA 1998, average Sunday attendance in all denominations added together should have been 15 per cent, whereas Peter Brierley's 1998 church census suggested a figure exactly half that.[1] Frankly, many of us may overestimate our churchgoing, just as we underestimate our eating and drinking! Yet, whichever method of calculating church attendances is used, both fit a pattern of slow overall decline, which has continued, almost without interruption, since the 1870s.

The contrast between the slow decline in churchgoing and the rapid decline in nominal membership is important. When questioned about their religious beliefs the British are by no means wholly secular. Only about a quarter claim to be atheists (albeit in the 1950s only a tenth did) and half claim to believe in life after death. A third also believe in religious miracles and see themselves as at least 'somewhat religious'. Two-thirds also think that 'there are basic truths in many religions'. In contrast, only 12 per cent responded that 'there is very little truth in any religion' and just 14 per cent that they were 'very' or 'extremely' non-religious.

Although the British are not exactly secular, there is evidence of increasing alienation from churches on moral issues. A generation ago many claimed that you do not need to go to church to be a good Christian. Today people may not consider being a Christian to be good at all. Despite considerable evidence that churchgoers are more active than others in voluntary work and see themselves as altruistic and unprejudiced, our public image is not so good. So in BSA 1998 three-quarters of respondents agreed that 'Looking around the world, religions bring more conflict than peace' and that 'People with very strong religious beliefs are often too intolerant of others.' And almost two-thirds agreed that 'Religious leaders should not try to influence government decisions.' Yet, somewhat confusingly, less than a third agreed that 'Britain would be a better country if religion had less influence.'

One moral area showing an increasing gap between official church teaching and popular attitudes is sex. BSA suggests that the public has remained consistently opposed to adultery (people clearly respect faithfulness), but has changed considerably in other areas. In 1983 a significant minority (42 per cent) considered premarital sex was 'not wrong at all'. By 1998 this had become a two-thirds majority, believing in addition that 'It's a good idea for a couple who intend to get married to live together first.' Interestingly, a majority of Anglican churchgoers agree. The instincts of the harshly treated report *Something to Celebrate*[2] were clearly close to the views of people within and outside the Church.

At Lambeth 1998, Western bishops were ambivalent about homosexuality (and remain so over Section 28), but non-Western bishops were overwhelmingly in favour of the strong line finally taken. Perhaps the former were conscious that attitudes are changing. BSA confirms this. In 1983, 62 per cent thought that 'sexual relations between two adults of the same sex' are always or mostly wrong, but only 45 per cent thought so in 1998. Across many Western countries most pensioners take this position, whereas the under-30s do not. Those of us who are middle-aged are simply confused! Given the average age of British congregations, the bishops' dilemma is obvious.

Naturally, church teaching on moral issues cannot simply be based upon social trends. Nazi Germany and Apartheid South Africa are clear warnings against that. Churches should risk unpopularity when resisting evil in society. However, the BSA results might help churches to be more aware of changing moral sensitivities. It is a matter of concern that so many ordinary people appear alienated from churches and may even feel morally superior to churchgoers. BSA 1998 suggests that most people are still morally concerned, agreeing, for example, that: income differences between rich and poor should be reduced; genetic science needs careful regulation; genetic research on humans should be only for therapeutic purposes; fiddling taxes is wrong; and personal honesty is important.

Generally we appear to be a decent and semi-religious lot. Yet, from the BSA evidence, we have less confidence in churches today than we have in the legal system or schools. Only Parliament ranks as low in our estimate. If a majority of the British population begins to feel moral superiority to churches, this is not good news for the long-term survival of these churches.

Public theology
1999

———•◆•———

As we edge into the new century a fascinating change is taking place in academic theology. Thirty years ago university theologians often feared that they might be the last of a genre. A more secular age would consider their work to be irrelevant and would question whether theology should be taught in universities at all.

Today, rather surprisingly, public theology (as it is sometimes termed) has received a new lease of life. Not only are theologians involved in a wide variety of public committees concerned with ethical issues arising from modern science, but they are also holding their own against scientific critics such as Richard Dawkins.

It is important not to exaggerate. There are still many scientists and non-scientists who agree with Richard Dawkins (author of, among other books, *The Selfish Gene*), especially when he claims that all religion is tantamount to magic causing irrational wars around the world. In contrast, they argue, science is based upon reason and, properly understood, contributes to a more rational and peaceful world. Dawkins was even rash enough to challenge Keith Ward, Regius Professor of Divinity at Oxford, assuming that he had no place in a university and would lose any public debate with him. When Keith Ward manifestly did not lose the debate that ensued,[1] Richard Dawkins changed tack by claiming that he was really a philosopher and not a theologian at all.

Against all odds there are now theologians on almost every national ethics committee related to scientific issues. For example, there is a theologian on the prestigious Nuffield Council on Bioethics, the Human Fertilisation and Embryology Authority (HFEA) ethics committee, the British Medical Association (BMA) medical ethics committee, on the ethics committees of the Royal

College of Gynaecologists and Obstetricians, the Royal College of Physicians, the Royal College of General Practitioners, and several other important bodies concerned with genetics in both humans and animals.

Cynics might claim that the theologians are there to give moral credence to these bodies. So long as they have a theologian as a member (albeit a sufficiently liberal theologian), then they can claim to have listened to (more conservative) religious voices and taken them into account. On this cynical analysis, including a theologian is just a way of silencing dissent. The sharp edges of fundamentalism can be controlled without being given any ground.

My own experience is quite the opposite. The committees that I belong to do expect me to be sympathetic to a variety of minority religious positions (both Christian and non-Christian). But what they really want from a theologian is someone who is a pastor and has a commitment to the vulnerable. They are often aware that philosophers are good at representing the purely logical issues involved (which I too must take fully into account), but can sometimes miss the pastoral issues. Of course, there are notable exceptions such as the philosophers Mary Warnock at Oxford, Stephen R. L. Clark at Liverpool and Gordon Graham at Aberdeen – all of them, as it happens, practising Anglicans and eminently pastoral. Yet theologians, if we are doing our job properly, are expected to be both logical and pastoral.

My former colleague at Edinburgh University, Duncan Forrester, illustrates this point well. This year he retires after 23 years as Professor of Christian Ethics and Pastoral Theology. He now serves on the Nuffield Council on Bioethics and has built a high reputation directing his own Centre of Theology and Public Issues at Edinburgh. Over the years he has engaged, through this Centre, with academics and practitioners in a wide variety of crucial areas, ranging from the medical, to the legal and penal, and to the economic and political. He has also written several important books on Christian ethics as it relates to the welfare state and social justice.[2] I well remember a residential conference he organized which involved Scottish politicians of the calibre of the late Donald Dewar. To my mind, Duncan Forrester has proved beyond doubt that the theologian can still be taken seriously in the public realm if he or she addresses crucial moral and pastoral issues with sympathy and intelligence.

It is one thing to claim that theologians can contribute on ethical issues – even those raised by modern science – but it is another to claim that they are now holding their own against scientific critics such as Richard Dawkins. Yet I believe that this is increasingly the case too. Ian Barbour in the United States and John Polkinghorne in Britain, both of them professional scientists and theologians, have succeeded in shifting the debate. In this country also, Gordon Dunstan and John Habgood have gained the respect over many years of leading scientists and doctors. More recently, the excellent historian and recently appointed Professor of Science and Religion at Oxford, John Brooke, and the Starbridge lecturer at Cambridge, Fraser Watts, have brought very considerable sophistication to the science and religion debate.

As a result, those who are properly informed are becoming increasingly aware that scientific reductionism is not the only way to view the world. It is perfectly possible to believe that this is a rational world (as science assumes) precisely because it is the work of a rational Creator. Indeed, the secularist assumption that this is a fortuitous world sits rather oddly with the presumption of rationality present within scientific methods and procedures.

None of this means that theology can assume its medieval position of prominence in the modern university. Personally, I hope that it never does. Theologians and church leaders have a bad track record of becoming oppressive when they assume positions of power.[3] We are far too strong-minded to be reliable politicians. However, it does mean that all is not lost. If theologians can engage with real public concerns, remain humble, pastoral and committed to the vulnerable, then I do believe that we have a role that will be valued in the twenty-first century – even within supposedly secular universities.

Gospel values and healthcare today

2001

Despite his first name and forebears, Wesley Carr is quintessentially Anglican. He takes the Bible very seriously, but not literally; he engages closely with the secular social sciences, while remaining distinctively theological; and he consistently searches for continuities between rationality and faith, especially in pastoral areas. Indeed, he concludes his *Handbook of Pastoral Studies* with the following conviction:

> It is . . . essential that pastors are familiar with the nature of the therapeutic approach. They will also discover that they have to work out their pastoral theology within that world without surrendering to it.[1]

This paper is written from a very similar conviction. As it happens, an earlier version was also first given at a seminar chaired by Wesley in the Deanery at Westminster Abbey.[2] My focus is specifically upon the distinctive contribution that a pastoral theologian might bring to modern bioethics.

In seeking to explore the distinctive contribution that a pastoral theologian might bring to modern bioethics I have been increasingly drawn to the healing stories in the Synoptic Gospels.[3] These stories, after all, represent the most abundant biblical resource on healing and seem to lie close to the centre of Jesus' own ministry. In the context of modern bioethics, however, it is possible that the 'miraculous' features of these stories are less relevant than the virtues that shape them. It may also be anachronistic to jump from practices in these stories to modern medical practice. Following Howard Clark Kee and Gerd Theissen,[4] I believe that the Synoptic healing stories should be understood in a first-century context before they are applied carefully to the twenty-first

16

century. And, following John Pilch's[5] biblical research using insights from medical anthropology, I am largely persuaded that these stories may have more to do with 'healing' than with 'cure' in the modern sense. Instead, using a method derived from qualitative research in the social sciences, I have sought to identify an ideal typology of virtues that shape the Synoptic healing stories as follows:

Four virtues occur most regularly within these stories. Compassion is the first of these, not because it is more frequent than the others but because it often comes at the beginning of a story. Occasionally the healing stories directly recount that Jesus was moved by compassion before healing someone. More often it is those to be healed or their friends or relatives who ask Jesus to show mercy or compassion. Sometimes the latter beg Jesus to respond. Compassion is also an important element within parables such as the merciful servant, the good Samaritan and the prodigal son, and is given by Mark as the initiating point for the feeding of both the four and the five thousand.

Care is a second distinctive virtue. This takes several forms. The most common of these forms is personal touching. An important part of many healing stories is Jesus touching the one to be healed, including touching those already labelled in the story as being 'unclean'. Many commentators identify this as ritual, even magical, action. However, from a perspective of healing, it may be viewed in more personal terms as the healer reaching out to care for the one who is to be healed but who has already been rejected by others as unclean. Another common form that care takes in the healing stories is anger. Sometimes Jesus appears to be angry at the illness or disability itself, sometimes Jesus 'sternly' warns those who have been healed not to tell others, but more often Jesus' anger is directed at religious authorities who place their principles (especially about keeping the Sabbath) before helping the one who could be healed. Care in this double sense – Jesus caring through personal contact with the vulnerable and unclean and Jesus passionately caring that they should be healed – is a strong feature of these stories.

Faith is a third distinctive virtue. Jesus often notes the faith of those to be healed or of their friends or relatives, and, conversely, can do little to help when there is an absence of faith. A recurrent conclusion he draws is that 'your faith has made you well'. On two occasions – the centurion's servant and the Canaanite woman – he particularly commends the faith of those who are not Jewish.

Reticence is a fourth virtue shaping the healing stories. A frequent end to healing stories in Mark, but also in places in Matthew (see especially Matt. 8—9) and Luke, is a command (in one place 'repeatedly') to the person healed to tell no-one. Not surprisingly, this feature has puzzled many biblical commentators. Even though the notion of some 'Messianic secret' is now largely discounted, its shadow still remains in many commentaries. Viewed from a perspective of healing it may appear rather differently. There are frequent mentions in the Synoptic stories of the amazement of the crowds at the healings, and alongside some of these are other indications that Jesus was anxious to withdraw from the crowds. Viewed as miraculous 'signs' – an occasional observation in the Synoptic Gospels but far more explicit in the Fourth Gospel – Jesus' healings could appear simply to be a dramatic demonstration of who he really was. Yet viewed as the healer reaching out to the ill and disabled with compassion, care and faith, a command to reticence is perhaps less surprising. It is the one concerned to demonstrate miraculous signs who needs crowds, not the one who is most concerned to heal the vulnerable. There may also be another reason for reticence in the healing stories, namely the related virtue of humility. There are direct and indirect references in a number of the healing stories to 'power' and 'authority', set in a wider framework of teaching about the kingdom of God. The healer who is conscious that it is finally God's power and rule that is at work in healing has good cause to feel personally humble.

Set in a wider context of religious ethics, all four of these virtues – compassion, care, faith and restraint – could be claimed by Judaism, Christianity and Islam alike. These virtues characterize Jesus as a Jew. According to Kee and Theissen, it is only their setting in a wider apocalyptic context within the Synoptic Gospels that differentiates them from contemporary Judaism. Again, although healing is not such a strong feature of the Qur'an, these four virtues are very characteristic of the Qur'an's sense of how good

Muslims should behave: all Suras but one begin with 'In the name of God, the Merciful, Compassionate'; followers of Jesus are specifically commended for their 'kindness' and compassion; care for the poor and vulnerable, especially through giving alms, is a clear requirement for Muslims; faith is evident throughout the Qur'an; and humility is required of those who remember that it is God who created them.

The virtue of compassion makes possible a double critique: of much secular bioethics for not making compassion sufficiently explicit, and of a number of Christian versions of bioethics for failing to place compassion before principles. Compassion, properly understood, is an essential starting point for bioethics even within a pluralistic society. Within the Synoptic healing stories compassion is not simply about feeling sorry for the vulnerable, nor is it even just about empathy, a preparedness to identify with the vulnerable. Rather, compassion is both a response to the vulnerable and a determination to help them.[6] In the Synoptic stories the vulnerable beg and cry for mercy and Jesus responds and acts. In many of the stories it is compassion and mercy that initiates the process of healing.

Within secular bioethics, a proper attention to the role of compassion may help to narrow the moral gap between personal resonance and a shared understanding of cosmic order. Even within a pluralistic society there may in reality be more common ground on compassion than is sometimes supposed. It is notoriously difficult to find agreement on common goods within a pluralistic society (as critics of natural law have often maintained), but it may be somewhat easier to agree upon common ills. So even if people cannot agree about what constitutes 'well-being', most might agree about what generally constitutes illness or disability and that, other things being equal, it is desirable to find ways of reducing or eliminating them. Of course, there will still be some areas where agreement remains elusive – for example, whether blindness constitutes a disability within blind families – but these areas are vastly outnumbered in modern society by areas of general agreement. Whether this agreement is entirely the result of cultural determinants or whether it is based, at least in part, in human nature need not be resolved here. It is sufficient that there is general agreement that it is desirable to reduce or eliminate illness and disability. Here there does seem, even within a pluralistic society, to be a general agreement that is not simply the result of personal resonance.

Compassion as a virtue is, however, more than a general agreement that it is desirable to reduce or eliminate illness and disability. It is both a response to the ill and disabled and a determination to help them. An approach to bioethics based only upon the widely used four bioethics principles of autonomy, justice, non-maleficence and beneficence championed by Beauchamp and Childress[7] might miss this. In my view these four principles do indeed suggest criteria to be considered carefully within the context of medical intervention, but they do not denote what drives and motivates that intervention in the first place. Behind the principles there is an implicit assumption that medical professionals should indeed respond to the ill and disabled and be determined to do their very best to help them.

The term 'care' is already widely used in secular medical contexts, for example in the term 'healthcare' itself, in 'community care' and 'care assistants'. It has been seen that in the Synoptic stories Jesus both cared through personal contact with the vulnerable and unclean and passionately cared that they should be healed. Both of these senses remain in these secular uses of the term 'care'. The healthcare professional is permitted and even expected to risk personal (but not intimate) contact with those who are ill and has a duty to do everything appropriate to cure them (if possible) or to reduce their pain or discomfort (if not). Care involves a range of core personal values, including competence, integrity, responsibility and confidentiality. Total patient care may also involve advocacy on behalf of the vulnerable and non-competent patient.

Care in this sense is particularly demanding and highlights the gap between moral demands and human propensity to selfishness. In secular care, one method adopted to ensure that adequate care is provided to patients is to produce written codes of professional practice and another is to have regular and systematic audits of actual practice. However, such methods fall short of ensuring care, because care, properly understood, involves a personal relationship between a carer and a (conscious) patient. Written codifications and the written track records essential to audit, although important and certainly not to be denigrated, nevertheless tend to set out or test the minimum conditions for professional practice rather than the personal and passionate care characterized in the Synoptic healing stories. Nonetheless, there remain important features of secular medicine today which explicitly (and many more implicitly) contain care in the latter sense. The hospice movement is an obvious example. It is, however, an example that raises the question whether such a movement could have arisen without having religiously committed founders.

What about faith in bioethics today? Particularly important here is the growing empirical evidence that there is a connection between religious belonging and health.[8] This suggests that religious belonging is a significant (but often ignored) independent variable in promoting physical and psychological health. Of course, there is still much debate about the causal factors involved here, yet it does seem that people with strong religious affiliations are more likely than others to have a sense of purpose in life and to be altruistic[9] and it is possible, in turn, that such motivation may have important implications for physical and psychological health.

There are two obvious problems with this evidence. The first is that, from a theological perspective, it suggests a rather instrumental understanding of faith: faith is treated as something that is beneficial for health rather than as a virtue that is good in itself. It is important to state very carefully that this is not the intention here. Rather, it may be an indication that well-being at different levels may be inter-connected. The second problem here is that the evidence is based upon a very generalized understanding of 'faith': many different forms of religious (or perhaps even secular) faith, some mutually contradictory, may be beneficial for motivation or health. In response, it may be noted that faith in the Synoptic healing stories is itself quite varied: sometimes it refers to the faith of the person to be healed; sometimes it is the faith of the relatives or friends; sometimes it appears to be faith in Jesus as healer; sometimes it seems to be faith in God; sometimes faith appears to be belief; sometimes it seems rather to be trust; sometimes it is the faith of fellow Jews; sometimes that of Gentiles.

Accordingly, the relationship of faith to healing can be analysed at a number of levels. The most basic of these is that of faith in the healing relationship. Without at least some trust in the medical professional – or, better, a mutual confidence between patient and professional – then healing may well be imperilled. Faith in the form of trust (but not always mutual confidence) was often present in the paternalistic medical practice, itself dependent upon patient compliance, of a previous generation. Within a context today that highlights patient autonomy and rights (without corresponding responsibilities) this trust may be weakened. The healing relationship understood in terms of mutual confidence offers a model of faith which respects both patient and professional autonomies and seeks to relate the two to each other.

The second level is concerned with the implicit assumptions of the healer him- or herself. Paul Halmos's seminal book *The Faith of the Counsellors*[10] noted that secular counsellors tend to depict their role in 'scientific' terms and, in the process, ignore value-commitments that are also fundamental to good counselling. Writing from a secular perspective himself, Halmos even suggested that it is the Christian virtue of care or *agape* which is the (usually unacknowledged) essential feature of effective counselling. It might be argued that a very similar case can be made within medical practice more generally.

The third level concerns specifically religious faith. Set within the context of the other two levels, faith in this sense can be seen as belonging to a continuum within the healing process. While healing is still possible without this level being made explicit, elements of it are likely to be implicit within many healing contexts. It is also at this level that the moral gap between the demand of moral duty and human propensity to selfishness can be narrowed. For the medical professional, especially when grounded in a worshipping community, faith in this third sense offers a powerful source of motivation to act selflessly.

Finally, there is reticence or humility within modern bioethics. In a context of exaggerated claims made in the name of medical (especially genetic) science and seemingly unlimited patient demand, this fourth virtue is particularly apposite today. Within medicine, humility in a moral sense is to be distinguished from etiquette. In terms of etiquette it is good manners not to boast about being able to do something even when there are grounds for believing that it can be done. However, as a moral term 'humility' involves a proper recognition both of personal frailty and of the role of others in achieving something. For the medical professional there is a constant temptation to claim too much authority and knowledge (a temptation in which patients themselves frequently conspire). A recurrent pattern in the Synoptic Gospels involves excessive pressure upon Jesus from crowds seeking healing and Jesus himself withdrawing from these crowds and warning most of those healed to tell no-one. Viewed from a theological perspective the medical professional has very clear reasons for not taking all the credit for any particular act of healing.

In a need- rather than demand-led health service, patient reticence is a crucial ingredient. To work properly such a health service does require patients to realize that there are others who are in need and possibly in greater need than themselves. For example, a system of rationing or prioritizing that is not simply based upon a patient's social status or ability to pay does require a shared sense of equity and fairness. The secular economist Amartya Sen's notion of 'equality of basic capability' is important here – especially his contention that moral perception is inextricably involved in an adequate understanding of equality and inequality in the world. An equality of basic capability, whether applied to the health service or more widely to society at large, involves qualitative issues and not simply a quantitative provision to satisfy basic needs. Douglas Hicks[11] argues that, once this is acknowledged, Christian ethics can contribute at three distinctive levels. First, it provides a moral vision and justification for how inequality matters and why public response is needed. Then it can offer moral examples of Christians who have actively striven against inequality. And, third, Christian ethics provides a particularly compelling moral call to action: at best, Christian communities can transform lives and behaviour towards a greater equality of capability.

Properly understood, I believe that the four distinctively religious virtues of compassion, care, faith and humility complement rather than conflict with the four bioethics principles of autonomy, justice, non-maleficence and beneficence. It is right that compassion should impel medical professionals to care for those in need and that, in turn, care should involve both caring about and caring for those who become patients. A proper understanding of the relationship between medical professionals and their patients also requires them to pay attention to non-maleficence, beneficence and the autonomy of these patients – and, in turn, for patients also to respect their autonomy. Faith is involved in some sense in the healing relationship between both parties and, for some, also between them and God. Justice is also an essential consideration in the broader context of health in society at large. And finally, humility should restrain both medical professionals from making exaggerated claims and patients from making selfish demands.

The Human Rights Act
2001

———•◆•———

It is just over a year since the Human Rights Act came into force in England and Wales, and earlier still in Scotland. At the time there was much speculation in newspapers that it would allow fringe groups to exploit the law. In the Church it received at best a muted welcome.

In the event these fears seem to have been misplaced (as they were previously in Scotland). In a wide-ranging review, the leading public law specialist, Michael Beloff QC, concluded that decisions resulting from the Act have been relatively conservative and that 'out of the 600-plus cases at the level of High Court and above in which Human Rights Act points have been taken in year one, the success rate has been of the order of only 15 per cent'.[1]

Two high-profile cases, both with important moral implications, illustrate this point. The first is the Diane Pretty case. In an article for *Church Times* written before her case was heard,[2] I argued that Christians should show compassion for her terrible predicament. She is in an advanced state of motor neurone disease and wants to die with dignity at some point soon, but is unable physically to do so without assistance. Her lawyers argued that the Human Rights Act gives her the right to be helped to die as she wishes and that her husband should be guaranteed immunity from prosecution if he does so.

Although I believe that she and her husband should be given as much leniency as possible (he would almost certainly not be punished with or without the Act), her case raises important questions about precedent for others. There is a real fear that a change in law in this area may create very serious problems for other vulnerable and disabled people. Nor is it clear that the Human Rights Act is relevant to her case, since it specifies rights to life and against inhuman treatment but not a right to be helped to die. The court judgment has now confirmed this.

In the other case, an initial judgment concluded that the rights of asylum seekers were infringed by their enforced detention while their cases were still under consideration. Yet, following the traumatic events of September 11, 2001, this decision has been reversed on appeal. For some this is an understandable reversal, given a need to protect society at large beyond upholding the freedom of individuals. For others it is a cynical reversal resulting from fears of massive compensation for all those asylum seekers detained in the past. Recently, another leading lawyer, David Pannick QC, has argued that by neglecting individual rights in our bid to counter terrorism we are in danger of ceasing to be the sort of society that we are supposed to be protecting. He also argues that it is not just in good times that we need the Human Rights Act but in times of crisis as well.

This last point raises crucial questions for the Church. For many years following the French Revolution there was a strong aversion, especially within the Roman Catholic Church, to the concept of human rights. It was seen as an essentially secular, if not anti-religious, concept. However, Pope John XXIII dramatically reversed this position by using the language of rights together with that of responsibilities in Encyclicals. According to this understanding all human beings, whatever their condition, have basic and equal rights. Yet in turn (unless they are babies or seriously disabled) they also have correlative duties or responsibilities. So we each have a right to life but also a duty to protect the life of others.

Alongside the introduction of human rights at a legal level, the present government has also used the moral language of rights and correlative responsibilities. I believe that it is time for the Church to give the government more credit for doing so. Instead of regarding the Human Rights Act as a potential threat, the Church should regard it in more positive terms. After all, it seeks to protect people in their religious and family lives as well as in their civic lives. If legal rights are properly balanced by a moral concern for the rights of others and a correlative duty to protect them, then this should be welcomed.

There is another point that Christians would be wise to note. The Franciscan Kieran Cronin, in his significant book *Rights and Christian Ethics*,[3] argues that rights can act as an important protection against other people's principles. Writing as a Roman Catholic, he is only too aware that his own Church in the past has persecuted people holding sincere principles at odds with its own. Following September 11, 2001, this point has become highly relevant again. A world that is constrained by a framework of universal human rights should be safer for all of us. Those with strong religious convictions have a bad track record of attempting to impose their own principles upon others.[4] Instead of seeking to persuade others through word and example (as Jesus himself did), they have too often resorted to state or local coercion to achieve this. In previous centuries church attendance, for example, was required either by the state or by employers and, even in the present, Sabbath restrictions have been upheld by church leaders. Today restrictions imposed upon Christians in some Islamic countries offer another shocking example.

Of course, human rights enshrined in legislation can never offer a sufficient framework to cover all aspects of human behaviour. When the Human Rights Act was introduced, a number of philosophers correctly pointed out that a comparison of different national and international versions of human rights reveals many tensions and perhaps contradictions. There is a real need for ongoing international discussion and dialogue here across different cultures and religious traditions. Nor can such legislation ensure moral responsibility on the part of citizens: it is no substitute for the persuasive capacity of faith, culture and tradition.

Yet, properly understood, legislation such as the Human Rights Act is an attempt to provide a framework in which all can live and co-operate peacefully as human beings.

The Mental Capacity Bill

2005

The Mental Capacity Bill is wending its way through the Parliamentary system.[1] The draft bill was published last year and discussed widely by various religious and secular bodies. Then the Joint Scrutiny Committee of the House of Commons and House of Lords published its report. In February this year the government published its response to this report. Now there is a short period of clarification, with the intention of the bill being presented to Parliament before the summer break.

I believe that the Church should welcome the key elements in this bill. It offers important safeguards for people when they are at their most vulnerable, either because they temporarily lack mental capacity or because they are mentally incapacitated with no prospects of recovery. The healing ministry of Jesus was specifically focused upon the vulnerable, such as the poor man who day and night 'among the tombs and on the mountains . . . was always howling and bruising himself with stones' (Mark 5.5). The Church cannot but be involved in the process of helping this bill to protect such vulnerable people.

However, there are three areas in the draft bill where the Church needs to be especially vigilant: the withholding or withdrawing of nutrition or hydration of those permanently lacking any mental capacity, advance directives (so-called living wills), and research on those lacking mental capacity. Some Christians, of course, regard the first as tantamount to involuntary euthanasia. But this was not the position taken by the bishops at the Lambeth Conference. The latter were clearly aware of potential abuse in both of these areas. Yet they did conclude that medical treatment or intervention (including artificial forms of nutrition or hydration) can legitimately be withheld from those in

28

a PVS. Given this, it does seem right that advance directives of competent individuals, indicating their wishes about withholding or withdrawing in advance of their becoming mentally incapacitated, should be respected by others.

Yet the experience of the Church of England in the 1960s suggests that there is a need for careful scrutiny even of well-intentioned bills. Then the Church gave cautious support for a change in the law on abortion, but the subsequent interpretation of the Abortion Act soon showed that what was thought by the Church to be a compassionate measure allowing abortion in exceptional circumstances became a law in effect allowing for abortion on request (at least in the first trimester). Similarly, clarification is still needed in the present bill.

1 *Withholding or withdrawing of nutrition or hydration.* The government is not proposing to change the status quo of judicial scrutiny for PVS patients, despite pressure from a number of secular bodies to do so. All PVS patient cases will still go to a Court of Protection when withdrawal is proposed. However, there are two caveats. The first is that (in line with the original legal judgment) this could change at some point in the future.[2] The second is that the withholding or withdrawing of nutrition or hydration from non-PVS patients is not currently protected in this way. I fear that there are as yet insufficient safeguards in the draft bill to protect non-PVS patients in situations when doctors and relatives might agree on a course of action that is against the best interests of patients.

2 *Advance directives.* We do need to know more about how the vulnerable are to be protected in this area too. Up-to-date decisions of competent people who have made a settled and informed choice not to have treatment surely should be honoured (most people today, Christians and non-Christians alike, would expect this for themselves). However, very clear safeguards are needed in this area, as well as some way of auditing that these safeguards are being adhered to. At present the bill lacks clarity about these safeguards.

3 *Non-therapeutic research on those lacking mental capacity.* Here it seems to me that the bill will have to give clear examples

and conditions, showing why non-therapeutic research can legitimately be done on patients who lack mental capacity. This will require very careful explanation indeed because it really does pull against the grain of the draft bill (which is concerned with protecting the vulnerable, not with using them for research that has no benefit to them).[3]

The Voluntary Euthanasia Society (VES) is using the first area in its current campaign. Len Doyal and I debated this at a recent BMA conference. His argument was as follows: the withdrawal of life-sustaining treatment from permanently incompetent patients differs little morally from involuntary euthanasia (except that it prolongs possible suffering); it is already acceptable and allowed in Britain, so why is voluntary euthanasia not allowed as well? My response was: his point is that, if we allow *a* then why do we not allow *b* (which is very similar), and if we then allow *b* why not *c* as well? But another way of framing this argument is to say that the law must always draw a line at some point, and at the moment it is drawn between *a* and *b* (i.e. between allowing withdrawal or withholding in some circumstances and allowing intentional killing). Of course, the line could be moved (to after *b* or even after *c*), but that should only be done if we can be confident that the cost to the vulnerable and the common good will be less than if we left the line where it is at the moment.

Given this wider debate, it is really important to keep insisting (and for the bill to insist) that the withdrawal of life-sustaining treatment from PVS patients is not involuntary euthanasia. It is about not artificially extending human life beyond the point that most of us consider acceptable. The Roman Catholic Church may also be moving to this position. Of course, pressure groups such as the Society for the Protection of Unborn Children (SPUC) resist it strongly. But there is already evidence of disquiet among a number of key Roman Catholics with the SPUC position if it is pushed into the area of PVS. Insisting upon the indefinite preservation of PVS patients through continuous medical intervention would appear both uncaring and unnecessary. It also seems to be a long way from Jesus' own ministry of healing.

Part 2

GENETICS AND STEM CELLS

The new genetics
1997

———•◆•———

Two recent cases have raised sharp ethical questions about the new genetics. First there was the ruling by the Association of British Insurers that people applying for life insurance *are* to be required to disclose information they might have from genetic screening. The Association also made clear that in two years' time they might require some individuals wishing to be insured to have genetic tests.[1] And then, within days, came the extraordinary news that a group of Scottish scientists had successfully cloned a lamb from an adult sheep – with the clear implication that human cloning will soon be a very real possibility. Many Christians will fear that the insurers and scientists together are 'playing God'.

The unusual features of genetic screening, as distinct from other forms of screening, are that: (a) genetic screening may have direct implications, especially when single-gene defects are detected, for other members of the patient's family; (b) there is at present little that can be done to remedy defective genes; (c) the health implications of many defective genes (with the exception of single-gene defects) are at present only partially understood. As a result of genetic screening, patients may thus be given information about their genetic inheritance, which they can do little or nothing about, whose health implications are often unclear, but which are likely to involve other members of their family.

In 1993 a Nuffield Council on Bioethics report, *Genetic Screening: Ethical Issues*, argued that there is a very real possibility of insurance and employment abuses here. Many people might be disadvantaged, especially since insurance companies might tend to be over-cautious even about those genetic defects whose effects are largely unknown (indeed, some genes which insurance companies in the West might regard as 'defects', such as the sickle cell gene, may actually be advantageous in different environments). Only a small number of people with a known family history of single-gene defect, who then test negative themselves, would benefit from such genetic screening.

The report advised against insurance companies requiring genetic tests and also called for a temporary moratorium on requiring the disclosure of genetic data, unless individuals already have a known family history of genetic disease or are seeking a large policy. However, it was always unlikely that insurance companies would ignore genetic data for long. Yet, as a result of being genetically screened, individuals may make discoveries about their genes, which they are powerless to change, which they barely understand, but which still disadvantage them in terms of insurance and house-buying. A concern for the vulnerable and disadvantaged is a crucial theological consideration here. It is not simply the wealthy who rely upon insurance. Housing, pensions and parts of healthcare are increasingly being covered by insurance. If the disclosure of genetic data also enters employment, then the vulnerable will be disadvantaged several times over. An aid to better healthcare will ironically have become another means of discrimination against the vulnerable.

The extraordinary case of the newly cloned sheep raises even deeper worries. Fundamental to this is a fear about modifying human origins, as in both the newer forms of human fertility treatment and emerging possibilities of germ-line surgery. Many people react intuitively with a sense of horror at reports, for example, about post-menopausal women being enabled to become pregnant,[2] or about the future possibilities of human reproductive cloning or gene modification.[3] They often use language about humans 'playing God' or about 'fabricating human beings'. They imagine that the scientist will increasingly replace the father, or even the mother, in producing babies . . . along the lines of Aldous Huxley's famous parody, *Brave New World*. And they fear that children will forfeit their sense of personal identity and that 'parenting' will become too mechanical.

This generalized fear is often held paradoxically alongside a deep concern to help potential parents who are seriously disadvantaged. Perhaps it is a concern for childless couples who are desperate to have children of their own, and yet who find that even adoption is increasingly rare in a world which no longer stigmatizes single parents. Or perhaps it is a concern to eliminate the more egregious single-gene diseases – knowing that genetic counselling or screening is never fully effective since a desire to have babies can often overcome even known serious familial risks.

In 1970 the theologian Paul Ramsey wrote in his powerful and prophetic book *Fabricated Man* that new fertility treatments and genetics tend to distort God's creation:

> To put radically asunder what God joined together in parenthood when He made love procreative, to procreate from beyond the sphere of love (artificial insemination with donor, for example, or making human life in a test-tube), or to posit acts of sexual love beyond the sphere of responsible procreation (by definition, marriage), means a refusal of the image of God's creation in our own.[4]

He argued emphatically: 'Men ought not to play God before they learn to be men, and after they have learned to be men they will not play God.'[5]

Yet the logic of Paul Ramsey's position might seem to be that humans should always accept what is there in the biological world as simply God-given. God has ordered sexuality and procreation in this way, so in this way it must remain. Those who reject any form of barrier or hormonal contraception (Ramsey was not among them) would seem to accept this proposition more strongly than those who do not. Yet even the former seldom apply this principle to the non-human biological world. Those viruses which are dangerous to human beings, for example, are seldom treated as God-given. Indeed, much of modern medicine would seem to go against such a principle.

An obvious reason for wariness in this area is the potential for political and social abuse. Memories still survive of the eugenic programmes of a number of totalitarian regimes. Real caution is needed in a liberal democracy to ensure that techniques developed for humanitarian reasons do not become instruments of political abuse in other regimes. There is even a danger in a liberal democracy that an understandable popular desire for 'perfect babies' does not become a means of discriminating against those with severe disabilities.

There are also very real physical risks involved in such treatment. Yet once they are understood and minimized from experience in the agricultural world, then I believe that it would be right to consider germ-line surgery strictly for those families who would otherwise face grave genetic disabilities. Scientists may still be some way from establishing the necessary genetic knowledge (and there must be considerable doubt about the applicability of all agricultural knowledge to humans) or from being able to undertake human genetic surgery. However, the cloned sheep brings this nearer. Indeed, it is possible to foresee an eventual change in regulation and practice in this area. For example, it might become possible safely to eliminate a deficient gene from sperm before implantation.[6]

I believe that it will be important to establish strict ethical criteria in this area. Three conditions are particularly important: (a) the condition is life-threatening; (b) the risks are broadly established (this is likely to be easier for single-gene than for poly-genetic conditions); (c) there is no safer alternative treatment. In short, this is a compassionate option: it is not an option to be made generally available for cultural, social or political reasons.

Given these strict conditions, Christians might cautiously welcome the newly cloned sheep and yet continue to warn most people of the dangers of genetic screening.

Allowing embryonic stem-cell research
2001

In contrast to a number of Christian ethicists, I believe[1] that we should give a cautious but genuine welcome to the prospect of stem-cell research for therapeutic purposes and to the Donaldson Report.[2] Although some caution is needed, Christian ethicists sometimes forget that there is the prospect of real good for very vulnerable people emerging from this research. Sometimes genetic scientists are pictured in demonic terms and their work is decried as being deeply destructive of the natural order. I do not share this position at all and am convinced that the aims of the stem-cell research envisaged in the Donaldson Report are fundamentally beneficent. Anyone who has pastoral or personal contact with those suffering from, say, Parkinson's or Alzheimer's disease will surely wish to find a cure and will welcome scientists who are attempting to do this. Where people differ is not usually about the ends of this research but about the means.

Some Christian ethicists are undoubtedly convinced that, since the early stages of stem-cell research involve the creation and subsequent destruction of embryos, then this research is intrinsically wrong whatever therapeutic benefits it promises. I respect this position – it is, after all, held by many deeply religious people – but I do not hold it myself. Others will argue on a purely utilitarian basis that the therapeutic advantages of stem-cell research simply override any scruples about human embryos or fears about human reproductive cloning. Again, this is not my position. What I will argue more cautiously is that our duties towards the sick and vulnerable (which I take to be at the heart of Jewish and Christian ethics) should finally be given priority over our duties towards those embryos that should never be implanted. Yet, since we also have a duty to society at large (a duty which is fundamental to

Jewish, Christian and indeed Islamic ethics), we should be properly cautious about research that may pave the way for others to do something which is intrinsically wrong: namely, to attempt to clone human beings.

The Donaldson Report acknowledges that, in the early stages at least of stem-cell research, it will be important to create cloned embryos using cell nuclear replacement (CNR) in order to provide stem cells that are suitable for therapy. Even if at some point in the future it may be possible to rely entirely upon adult cells, initial research will involve the creation and then destruction of CNR embryos. For those who believe that any embryo from the time of fertilization should be accorded the same right to life as a baby or as an adult, this procedure clearly involves the deliberate killing of an innocent human being. It is therefore intrinsically wrong and stem-cell research, if it depends upon this in the initial stages, is itself intrinsically wrong.

It is important to consider carefully this objection to stem-cell research. It is held by quite a number of conservative Jews, Christians and Muslims and occasionally by secular people as well. In essence it maintains that human life begins at conception and should always receive our full protection. Other positions which seek to make distinctions between 'human life' and 'human persons' or between 'potential human persons' and 'full human persons' do seem to lack the clarity and logic of this conservative position. At conception genes are fused and gestation begins. According the embryo from the outset full protection presents an unambiguous moral position. In contrast, many other positions appear morally arbitrary, seeming to rely more upon convenience than upon principle.

Critics of this conservative position sometimes dismiss it too readily. Although I do not share it myself, I am grateful that it still has articulate defenders.[3] If nothing else, they force us to look carefully at the ethical implications of medicine and science involved in the beginning and end of human life. Yet despite the clear logic of this conservative position, it involves a sharp conflict with practical experience. In practice, most couples do not mourn the spontaneous loss of an early embryo as they do a baby who is near to term. Any clinician or pastor with experience of couples facing spontaneous abortions will be aware that perinatal death often involves a deep grieving process which early miscarriage typically does not. Indeed, up until the late nineteenth century the Roman Catholic Church itself made a clear distinction between early and late abortions, regarding early induced abortions as punishable only by a fine but late induced abortions as capital offences.

So what is the moral alternative? Obviously one could hold that embryos have no moral status whatsoever and that we have no corresponding moral responsibilities towards them. Some philosophers have argued that it is our ability to think which gives us moral status as human beings. Since embryos cannot think, they therefore have no such status. I cannot spend much time arguing against this position, but I do find it seriously deficient in two crucial respects: first, because it has very damaging implications for those with severe learning disabilities and for the elderly with reduced intellectual abilities; and second, because it privileges intellectual capacity. As a theologian I am highly suspicious of those intellectuals who claim that it is intellect alone – rather than, say, a capacity to be loved – that makes us truly human.

The Donaldson Report argues for 'a middle position', according to which 'the special status of an embryo as a potential human being is accepted, but the significance of the respect owed to developing human life is regarded as increasing in proportion to the degree of development of the embryo' (4.2). Like a number of other religious ethicists, I share this notion of progressive moral responsibility.[4] It does seem to match the practical experience mentioned earlier. Yet it lacks the moral clarity of the conservative position. It offers no clear guidelines about how much respect is required at each stage of development. Notwithstanding, it is on this basis that the Donaldson Report concludes that at the very early stages of development 'it is morally justified to use embryos for research purposes in order to benefit others, provided that such research is necessary and justified by the benefit it may produce in the long run' (4.2).

There are problems with this argument. Supposing it is found in the long run that there are no tangible therapeutic benefits from this research. Presumably then the ethicist must conclude that it was not after all morally justified. With purely consequential arguments you have to wait and see what the actual consequences are before you can decide whether something was morally justified. All that you can safely say in the present is that, if all turns out as you hope or expect, then you will be morally justified. But, of course, if it does not then you will not. Not a very satisfactory moral position. Or is it simply the *hope or expectation* that matters? As long as you hope or even expect that the research will yield therapeutic benefits, then it is morally justified . . . a sort of acting in good faith. Undoubtedly, acting in good faith is important for ethics (and indeed for theology), but the difficulty here is: do good-faith hopes or expectations outweigh the moral respect we should have for human embryos?

The Donaldson Report recalls that it was precisely the issue of research on embryos which divided the original Warnock Committee almost two decades ago. Nine members of that Committee argued in favour of such research (albeit with careful conditions) and seven dissented, including as it happens the only theologian on the Committee, my late colleague Professor Tony Dyson. Critics of the Donaldson Report will no doubt notice that it finally had no dissenters. So perhaps after a decade of research on embryos (a few of them deliberately created for research purposes) we have begun to lose our moral sensitivities in this area. So, just as we agonized about legalizing induced abortion in the 1960s, applying strict criteria at the time, and then largely stopped agonizing with the passing of time and some several million legalized abortions later, so now, it might be argued, we have become morally desensitized about creating and destroying human embryos for research.

Perhaps this is too harsh, but it does suggest that some caution is needed before we become too enthusiastic about research upon human embryos, regarding them as little more than expendable human tissue. The Donaldson Report certainly cannot be accused of such a view, but it is not difficult to see that a shift in consensus between Warnock and Donaldson might in the future be followed next by a shift in content towards the expendable-human-tissue position. Tony Dyson, who himself suffered from Parkinson's disease, was in most other respects a liberal theologian, but he feared at the time that we were crossing a line or, if you prefer, stepping onto a slippery slope. The Donaldson Report, when contrasted with the Warnock Report, may unwittingly provide critics with evidence that this is so.

The other troublesome ethical issue raised by the prospect of stem-cell research also involves a slippery slope, or, as I prefer to call it, procedural and moral deterioration. Creating embryos by cell nuclear replacement is the first step in human reproductive cloning. The Donaldson Report is well aware of this, but insists that the regulatory powers of the HFEA are sufficient to ensure that CNR embryos are never developed beyond 14 days and are never implanted. The report upholds a strict legal framework that allows CNR embryos to be created for therapeutic purposes alone and declares it illegal to attempt human reproductive cloning. Or to summarize this in language that the report dislikes, a firm line is drawn between therapeutic and reproductive cloning.

I, too, believe that this firm line should be drawn and so, I suspect, do most people. But the trouble is that even if it is drawn in Britain and the rest of Europe, will it be drawn elsewhere? More than that, the knowledge gained in Britain about human CNR will doubtless be very valuable elsewhere in the world to those determined to embark upon human reproductive cloning. In an age of morally responsible science, it is no longer sufficient to say 'knowledge is knowledge' and wipe our hands of any responsibility for how this knowledge might be used by the less scrupulous. I am convinced that attempts to clone human beings are intrinsically wrong, since it is always wrong to attempt risky interventions on human beings without their consent and with few if any obvious human benefits. If this is so, then stem-cell research using CNR embryos in Britain may pave the way for something intrinsically wrong to happen elsewhere in the world, namely attempting to clone human beings. It is not sufficient morally to say, as the Donaldson Report says, that Britain already has the kind of regulatory powers to stop such procedural or moral deterioration. In a global context Britain clearly does not and cannot have such powers.

So the caution in my welcome for the Donaldson Report is based upon two distinct fears. The first fear is that we may be becoming less and less sensitive to the propriety of creating embryos for research, and the second is that unwittingly we may be taking a step along the path to human reproductive cloning. I am not sure that the report, admirable as it is in many respects, adequately addresses these two fears. Indeed, I am not sure that I can adequately address the second fear myself. All technology is power and, in a global context, it can be used by good and bad people alike. This has been our persistent problem with nuclear technology and we are fast becoming aware that it is also so with information technology. It will surprise few of us to discover that genetic and medical science can similarly be used for beneficent and maleficent ends. Sadly, we may have to conclude that this is possibly so for well-intended stem-cell research as well.

However, on the first fear there is more to be said. There is a crucial difference between embryos cloned by CNR and non-cloned embryos, namely that it would be intrinsically wrong (given my earlier argument) to implant the former but not the latter. From a scientific perspective both could be implanted and might indeed be able to gestate to term. In this respect both differ from a vesicular mole which, although fertilized and alive, could never gestate to term. My distinction here is between 'could' and 'should'. CNR embryos could technically be implanted, but morally (and indeed legally) they should never be implanted. It is not simply that we do not intend to implant such embryos (as the report mentions) but that it would be *intrinsically wrong* to do so. In contrast, there is rarely any moral interdiction against implanting non-cloned embryos. Even in those rare cases of so-called 'saviour siblings', where it is considered preferable to implant one embryo rather than another, it is not morally forbidden for any non-cloned embryo to be implanted (even an embryo with some genetic disability). At most we are talking about moral preferences here. A family wants to have a baby who could save a sibling's life rather than a baby who could not. Or a family with a monogenetic condition would prefer to have a baby without that condition to one with it. However, with CNR embryos it is intrinsically wrong to implant even though it is technically feasible. This is not a moral preference but a moral interdiction.

If this is so, then our duties towards a CNR embryo are distinctly less than our duties towards a non-cloned embryo. From a moral (and perhaps legal) perspective a CNR embryo is never a potential baby. As a result it would not be appropriate, as some Christian ethicists have claimed, to accord it the sort of respect that we should give to a potential baby. Indeed, given a choice between medical research upon animals that involves them in pain and research upon a CNR embryo, then I would reluctantly choose a CNR embryo (or, if possible, human tissue). My reluctance here is based less on the status of such an embryo than its link to human reproductive cloning.

It is our duty to help sick and vulnerable people which convinces me finally that this is morally justifiable research. If my argument is correct, then we need to be vigilant about the path that could lead to human reproductive cloning. Yet we do not have a duty to treat CNR embryos themselves with the same moral respect as non-cloned embryos. Furthermore, our duty towards sick and vulnerable people is overwhelmingly more significant than any minimal duty we may have towards CNR embryos. Using such embryos wisely to develop stem-cell therapy does seem to be morally justified.

Blocking embryonic stem-cell research

2006

President Bush has used his veto to block US federal funding for embryonic stem-cell research.[1] The Senate recently passed the Stem Cell Research Enhancement Act by 63 votes to 37. Justifying this first use of his presidential veto, he argued: 'This Bill would support the taking of innocent human life in the hope of finding medical benefits for others. It crosses a moral boundary that our society needs to respect, so I vetoed it.'

For the last four years I have served as a member of the Medical Research Council's Stem Cell Bank Steering Committee. This is the committee responsible for monitoring and drawing up criteria for the importing, banking and use of embryonic stem cells for research into serious medical conditions. Richard Harries, when Bishop of Oxford, also chaired the House of Lords Committee that endorsed such use of embryonic stem cells.[2] Clearly, if President Bush is right, then Richard Harries and I have crossed a moral boundary by endorsing 'the taking of innocent human life'.

President Bush, like the Pope and his predecessor, is committed to a strong form of vitalism that sees a moral equivalence between the life of an early embryo and an adult suffering from a degenerative condition such as Parkinson's. From this perspective, full human life begins at conception and it is simply wrong to kill one human being (even an embryo) in order to treat another human being.

Many theologians writing about embryonic stem-cell research today take a similar position. Among theologians, those of us who support such research appear to be in the minority. Indeed, we are frequently accused of succumbing to a purely secular understanding of human life.

However, it might be a moral equivalence position that raises the more acute theological problems, especially for the so-called problem of evil. In nature a majority of human conceptions either do not implant or are spontaneously aborted soon after implantation. A moral equivalence position commits us to believing that, since these conceptions are indeed human beings, then a majority of human beings die long before they are born. Apparently this is the world so disastrously ordered, or allowed to be, by an all-loving, all-knowing and all-powerful God.

Of course, there is a traditional theological response to this problem. Innocent human life that is unrewarded in this life will yet be rewarded in a future life beyond death. Human beings who were never implanted or who were spontaneously aborted in early pregnancy will still enjoy heavenly life. Yet this conclusion also raises difficulties. Heaven becomes extremely odd, since apparently it is peopled for the most part by human beings who have never been born.

Far from succumbing to secularism, my own support for the use of embryonic stem cells for research into serious medical conditions is based upon both pastoral theology and the Gospel healing stories.

A moral equivalence position involves a sharp conflict with pastoral experience [as already noted in the previous piece] . . . More positively, in the Gospel healing stories those with diseases and disabilities came again and again to Jesus begging for compassion, and he responded. This compassion is not simply about feeling sorry for the vulnerable, nor is it even just about empathy, a preparedness to identify with the vulnerable. Rather, compassion [as seen earlier] is both a response to the vulnerable and a determination to help them, sometimes at the expense of principled scruples. Quite reasonably, the leader of the synagogue pointed out that a woman crippled for 18 years did not need to be healed on the Sabbath. Yet Jesus, ignoring principled scruples about the Sabbath (and ritual impurity), denounced him and the surrounding crowd as 'You hypocrites' (Luke 13.15). This is strong teaching.

President Bush's statement mentions 'the hope of finding medical benefits for others'. The use of the word 'hope' is important here. Listening carefully to scientists has persuaded me that embryonic (rather than adult) stem cells offer the most hope of finding medical benefits. But it is hope, not certainty. There is no guarantee that stem-cell therapy will eventually be safe and effective. Yet, unless one holds a moral equivalence position, there are strong compassionate reasons for allowing this research. And the primary motivation of the research scientists I have met has indeed been compassion. Many of them have first-hand experience of the patient groups who hope fervently (as I do) that stem-cell therapy will one day work.

Human enhancement

2007

An advertisement for a well-known hearing aid currently claims: '*Now* you really will hear better than ever before.' So your hearing will not simply be restored to its former level (treatment), it will supposedly be improved beyond this (enhancement). Few of us may see much ethical difficulty in blurring this particular boundary between treatment and enhancement. Yet we might be more concerned in other areas. What about drugs taken to enhance, rather than restore, our athletic abilities or our powers of reasoning? What about mechanical implants, embryo selection, or even genetic engineering purely for human enhancement?

Perhaps we should stick with what is 'natural' and 'God-given'. Yet a small amount of thought soon raises problems. Spectacles might be labelled simply as treatment (and therefore allowable), but what about binoculars? After all, binoculars allow us to see beyond our 'natural' capacities. Similarly, computers allow us to calculate, cars and planes to travel, and telephones to communicate, beyond our God-given capacities. Few see ethical problems here.

The British Medical Association's Ethics Department has just launched a carefully balanced discussion paper, *Boosting Your Brainpower: Ethical Aspects of Cognitive Enhancements*.[1] It reaches few conclusions but raises many important questions. The bioethicist John Harris has also published a new book in this area, *Enhancing Evolution: The Ethical Case for Making Better People*.[2] In contrast to the BMA document, it is witty, opinionated and provocative. Taken together these two publications raise the profile of an emerging ethical debate. Should there be ethical and legal constraints to some (surely not all) forms of human enhancement? And, if so, how can these be made accurately and fairly?

47

This is a very confused and confusing area. Boundaries between treatment and enhancement are often difficult to draw and there is little prospect of any consensus on what is considered 'natural' (or even on whether treatment itself is 'natural'). John Harris uses his philosophical skills very effectively to expose public confusion here. At the outset he argues that few of us are opposed to schools that set out deliberately to improve the mental and physical capacities of their students. He then asks why we should oppose the use of drugs, embryo selection or genetic engineering to achieve the same ends. It is his conviction that we have a positive moral duty to enhance human beings, perhaps using any of these methods.

Harris is a robustly secular libertarian. He believes that those who would seek to disallow any form of human enhancement need 'to show not simply that it is unpopular, or undesirable, or undesired, but that it is seriously harmful to others or to society and that these harms are real and present, not future and speculative' (p. 74). Issues like global warming would not fare too well given this position, let alone concerns about future generations (as the joke goes, 'What have they ever done for us?'). I am not even sure that cruelty to animals would be disallowed using Harris's criteria.

What about performance-enhancing drugs in sport (or students taking cognition-enhancing drugs)? Harris is again robust. If consenting athletes wish to take them, then let them do so since they only harm themselves. Again, if people wish to have children using human reproductive cloning (following similar techniques to Dolly the sheep), then allow them to do so. Harris dismisses concerns about identity, pointing out correctly that identical twins, let alone conjoined twins, have much closer identities. As long as it is safe to do so, parents should be allowed to choose, just as they are allowed to do in the rest of life.

For many religious or secular humanists there is something dangerously misleading about John Harris (he is, after all, a member of the influential Human Genetics Commission). His arguments are habitually individualistic and lack any sense of the common good. Allowing athletes freely to take performance-enhancing drugs is likely to mean that in the future anyone wishing to be a successful athlete must also take them. Taking dangerous drugs will become an essential part of being an athlete. Individual athletes may have made free choices, but in the end all will have been harmed and athletics itself debased. It was for this reason that bare-knuckle boxing was banned and that gladiatorial games have long been considered deeply uncivilized.

Attempts at human reproductive cloning are likely to remain illegal in civilized countries for similar reasons: there is no very good reason for making such attempts; there are safer ways to prevent genetic disabilities; the embryo certainly has not given consent; and the risks are unknowable without unethical attempts. In the interests of the common good most countries agree that human reproductive cloning should remain illegal. And so far no country has bought into Harris's dictum that 'persons properly so-called are individuals capable of valuing their own existence' (p. 97) – a position that could legalize both infanticide and involuntary euthanasia of the chronically depressed. Perhaps not the best way to enhance the common good.

Less individualistic ethical thought is surely needed here. Religious and secular humanists should work closely to promote a wider and deeper ethical discussion based upon both compassionate care and common good.[3] Only in this way are we likely to tread wisely in this novel area of ethics.

Synthetic biology

2009

Exciting new developments in science and technology are raising fresh ethical challenges. The latest is in an area now called synthetic biology. In its most dramatic form synthetic biology offers the possibility of creating new forms of life not to be found anywhere in nature. A recent discussion paper for the Royal Society stated pungently that 'in essence it is about redesigning life'.

Synthetic biology does not simply re-order some natural components (as genetic engineering does), it attempts also to synthesize artificial components with living components in order to produce, for example, more efficient bio-fuels or personalized forms of medicine. Machines in the future might even contain 'living' components.

This novel area brings together the skills of computer modelling and advanced engineering with DNA mapping and synthesizing. Developed over the last decade, particularly in Boston and the Bay Area of California, it has now come to Britain. A Centre of Synthetic Biology has recently been established at Imperial College London with similar developments at Cambridge and Edinburgh universities.

The Royal Academy of Engineering has just published a report, *Synthetic Biology: Scope, Applications and Implications*,[1] which offers a state-of-the-art overview of this developing science. Encouragingly, the report also devotes a substantial chapter to the ethical and social implications of synthetic biology. It is excellent to see scientists addressing ethical issues ahead of a novel development. At stake are not just the usual questions about safety and intellectual property, but also more challenging ones about national security and the propriety of creating novel forms of life.

The immediate applications of synthetic biology do not appear to be particularly threatening. The Academy's report states that 'Synthetic biology aims to design and engineer biologically based parts, novel devices and systems as well as redesigning existing, natural biological systems' and argues that it could make important contributions to healthcare, agriculture, industry and even climate change.

The development of new drugs, for example, seems at first sight to be relatively unchallenging. An anti-malarial drug (artemisinin) has already been developed using synthetic biology and is likely to go into full production with huge potential for better health in many developing countries. In future, personalized drugs produced by synthetic biology may have less harmful side effects and be able to respond more 'intelligently' to the body's defence mechanisms.

But what if synthetic biology is used instead to produce harmful agents that can be used by terrorists? Garage technology in California already makes it possible for individuals (benevolent or malevolent) to experiment in this area without any formal control.

The Academy's report alarmingly states:

> In the US [biosecurity] is the most heavily debated social risk associated with synthetic biology . . . Biosecurity concerns were triggered by the synthesis of several pathogenic viruses, including the 1918 influenza virus and an infectious polio virus that was synthesized using only published DNA sequenced information and mail-ordered raw materials.

Three years ago a *Guardian* journalist in this country showed that he could order the DNA sequences for the smallpox virus and have them delivered to his home.

It is clear that great vigilance is needed. Sadly, technology, as the scientist–theologian Ian Barbour often reminded us, is in itself neither good nor bad – it is power that can be used or misused. Similarly, computers can be used for better communication between friends and families or they can be misused to download child pornography or to facilitate the perpetrators of September 11, 2001 and the 2005 London bombings. That is not a reason for abandoning computers, or now synthetic biology, but it is a reason for vigilance and, where possible, careful governance.

Another imminent use of synthetic biology is the production of new biomaterials. For example, people in the South Pacific have long used the silk of the orb spider web to make fishing nets and traps because it is both strong and light. Synthetic versions of this silk may soon be in full production and beneficial in many different areas. Aeroplanes, for example, would be more fuel-efficient and less damaging to the environment if they were lighter while remaining strong.

Yet producing synthetic forms of nature and, in turn, novel forms of life not actually found in nature raises unnerving questions about life itself. The first synthetic organism (a polio virus) was produced in 2002 by Cello and co-workers at the State University of New York. The Academy's report notes qualms of some about such a development: 'The creation of synthetic living organisms according to rational and reductionist engineering principles is likely to invoke worries about scientists "playing God", and some may object to synthetic biology at the outset for this reason.'

[As seen earlier] the theologian and ethicist Paul Ramsey accused scientists 40 years ago of 'playing God' in the early days of in vitro fertilization (IVF), and quite a number of theologians have made the same accusation against biotechnologists today. Yet most of modern medicine and all surgery could be banned if this accusation were taken too literally. Perhaps it is more appropriate to argue for ethical responsibility and to resist such theological hyperbole.

Synthetic biology does bring ethical challenges that do need to be addressed carefully and responsibly. It is encouraging that the Royal Academy is developing this discussion in Britain.

Part 3

ABORTION AND FERTILITY TREATMENT

Abortion dilemmas

1996

—————•◆•—————

Abortion has once again become a matter of public concern. Just when it seemed that Britain had accepted that abortion should be available on demand, three cases have uncovered considerable moral queasiness. First there was public concern about the destruction of thousands of frozen embryos. Then there was the selective abortion of a 16-week fetus because the mother apparently 'could not afford to have twins'. And now there is the dilemma of the woman who used unregulated fertility treatment to conceive octuplets. What has Christian ethics to say about all of this?

Of course, each of the cases is distinct. Yet together they illustrate one of the sharpest dilemmas of the twentieth century – technical power has advanced rapidly in all sorts of areas at a time of considerable moral confusion. In medicine this means that doctors are able to give us ever more startling choices at precisely the moment when we are less and less clear about the moral criteria needed to make these choices responsibly. The very skills of modern medicine in fertility treatment, IVF and surgical techniques of selective abortion have served to highlight this central dilemma. In theory such medical advances increase patient choice and autonomy. In practice they compound our moral confusions in a pluralistic age.

Even as Christians we are scarcely united. Some (probably a minority) are opposed to abortion on any grounds, regarding all induced abortions even at the earliest stage of conception as the murder of babies. On this basis the woman carrying octuplets is simply told to continue with her pregnancy, whatever the risk to her or to her babies. If she has been foolish enough to misuse fertility treatment, then she must live with the consequences. Others of us do accept that there are occasions when abortion is justified, especially in a case such as this, but are nevertheless uneasy about the way the Abortion Act is now widely interpreted. On compassionate grounds we accepted in the 1960s that abortion could be the lesser of two evils, but we soon discovered that early abortions had become available on almost any grounds. In the process [as noted earlier] a liberty had been turned into a licence. And other Christians again simply support what they regard as a more liberal and caring society.

When I was interviewed at the weekend for the *Sunday* programme on Radio 4, I was asked if there was anything distinctive that Christians, despite our differences, could say together on these difficult issues. Unfortunately owing to time constraints this side of the interview was omitted. Perhaps I can rectify this now. There are two important levels at which theology can contribute to this debate – the first is from a perspective of creation and the second from a specifically Christian perspective of redemption.

Those of us who believe in a God who creates and lovingly sustains us have this much in common – we believe that life is essentially God-given. I prefer this relational term 'God-given' to the more static concept of the 'sanctity of human life' or the less than Christian notion that life is 'sacred'. If we regard life, both human and non-human, as a gift, then we should be encouraged to respond with gratitude and responsibility. In prayer and worship we give thanks for the gift of life and are encouraged to recognize that this gift ought to be treated with respect. Even though we may still conclude that there are occasions when this gift can sometimes become an overwhelming burden (either at the beginning of life or at its very end), we must still treat it with deep respect.

Life regarded as God-given is quite different from a secular perspective. The writings of the Australian philosopher Peter Singer over the last decade illustrate this clearly. His recent book *Rethinking Life and Death*[1] has the instructive subtitle *The Collapse of Our Traditional Ethics*. Using a number of current legal judgments about the withdrawal of nutrition and hydration from persistent vegetative state patients and the increasing *de facto* acceptance of more direct forms of euthanasia as his starting point, he offers a sustained polemic against what he sees as the collapsing Judaeo-Christian ethical tradition. Replacing this tradition simply with individual self-awareness and rationality, he even justifies infanticide:

> In the modern era of liberal abortion laws, most of those not opposed to abortion have drawn a sharp line at birth. If, as I have argued, that line does not mark a sudden change in the status of the fetus, then there appear to be only two possibilities: oppose abortion, or allow infanticide. I have already given reasons why the fetus is not the kind of being whose life must be protected in the way that the life of a person should be. Although the fetus may, after a certain point, be capable of feeling pain, there is no basis for thinking it rational or self-aware, let alone capable of seeing itself as existing in different times and places. But the same can be said of a newborn infant. Human babies are not born self-aware, or capable of grasping that they exist over time. They are not persons. Hence their lives would seem to be no more worthy of protection than the life of a fetus.

Singer does retreat slightly from this conclusion – after all, a baby can no longer be viewed as a part of a woman's body – but only slightly. He does finally believe that infanticide can be ethically justified and is fully aware that this conclusion sharply challenges many forms of religious ethics.

Faced with such secularist polemics, religious traditions may appear increasingly distinctive. Singer and other secular thinkers tend to present their views as simply 'rational' and based on 'common sense'. In reality they are offering faith positions, albeit a secular faith. In contrast, the belief that life is God-given is shared by Christians, Jews, Muslims, Sikhs, and more vaguely by a majority of the population of Britain. Perhaps we should be prepared to challenge secular 'faith' whenever it is expressed by those defending abortion on demand, infanticide or involuntary euthanasia. A pluralistic society is not necessarily a purely secular society.

As Christians I believe that we can say more than this. Without claiming that we represent society as a whole, we can and should be offering a distinctive morality for others to follow. In the teaching of Jesus there is an overwhelming emphasis on the marginalized, the suffering and on those with disabilities. There is a very natural wish for parents to have perfect babies and for all of us to die in full command of our physical and rational powers. Yet there is a real danger of undervaluing the disabled in the process. In Christ we believe that these natural barriers are overcome. It was for this very reason that the 1965 Church of England report *Abortion: An Ethical Discussion,*[2] chaired by Ian Ramsey, defied public opinion at one crucial point. A Gallup poll in 1966 suggested that 71 per cent of the public supported abortion when 'the child may be born deformed' and 79 per cent when 'the health of the mother is in danger' (but only 33 per cent when 'the family does not have enough money to support another child'). Ramsey and his committee supported the grounds of the woman's physical and even psychological health, but worried deeply about what we are saying to the disabled if we accept fetal deformity *en bloc.* Of course, agonizing decisions remain and as Christians we are not immune. Yet our vision of life surely should encompass and include the abled and disabled alike. For us only Christ is perfect.

How do these principles apply to the three cases at the beginning of this article? My own view is that people were right to feel uneasy about the destruction of the frozen embryos. We should remind ourselves that even these primitive forms of human life are God-given. For me Cardinal Hume was right to say that, although he could see no alternative to unfreezing them, we should still treat them with respect. The selective abortion of a twin, solely on financial grounds, surely offended these principles. Abortion on purely financial grounds hardly treats life as God-given and is likely to discriminate particularly against the marginalized and disabled. On the other hand, the selective abortion of some of the octuplets may be a requirement of respecting the God-given life of both the mother and her babies. Continuing to term will apparently place her life in serious danger and put at risk all of the babies. She may be tempted to take this risk through a curious combination of financial inducements from a newspaper and anti-abortion principles, but I hope she does not.[3]

Drawing the line in fertility treatments

1998

———————•◆•———————

Where should we draw the line in novel human fertility treatments? Twenty years ago this summer, Louise Brown, the first IVF baby, was born. Yet, after more than 300 IVF births, one of Britain's leading IVF specialists, Professor Ian Craft, was quoted last week as saying that 'we have to draw the line somewhere'.

Professor Craft was responding to a report about a woman, after treatment at a private clinic in Italy, giving birth at the age of 60. He explained that at his clinic 'we have chosen 55 because that is the age of the oldest natural conception in Britain'. Despite drawing this particular line, the clinic apparently requires no external evidence of the age or domestic situation of a woman seeking IVF.

A week earlier a US fertility specialist, Dr Richard Seed, was in the news for announcing that he intends to provide human cloning as an option for childless couples. The only line he seems to draw is that of infertility itself. He is not proposing to offer cloning simply to satisfy scientific curiosity or personal whim, but as an option for cases of infertility. Yet he insists that, if federal law in the United States attempts to ban human cloning in private clinics, he will take his Chicago clinic south to Mexico. So, if infertile couples wish to have children, they should be free to have them without state interference . . . it is for them alone to draw lines.

Both Professor Craft and Dr Seed appear to be compassionate libertarians. A practising Methodist, Dr Seed is highly suspicious of government control over individual lives. Professor Craft, in turn, insists that 'there is no reason to disparage older women or discourage them from having children'.

Is human fertility treatment out of control? Even if there are local and enforced controls, the international IVF market surely means that women in their sixties and even seventies may increasingly be enabled to have children (provided they have the money – this is no option for the poor). Despite widespread government bans, human cloning will surely happen somewhere in the world. Sheep and now cattle have already been cloned, so human reproductive cloning has become a real possibility. The new genetics also offers the not-too-distant prospect of genetic surgery – of human germ-line surgery. Just as the genetic inheritance of plants, of vegetables and now of animals can be changed, so this may soon become an option for humans too. In the process it might be possible to eliminate some of the most egregious human genetic diseases. Although still banned in Britain, there is also the prospect of using human genes in animals to increase the supply of vital organs for transplants (xenografts). Perhaps one day it will be possible to create babies who will grow up but will no longer age, or babies with super brains, or . . .

In the New Year I attended a large conference of Christian ethicists in Atlanta who discussed many of these issues. Some believed that all such attempts erode the vital difference between God and human beings, between the infinite and the finite, and between created and manufactured life. Others argued that we should not rule out of court novel possibilities for human procreation without compelling reasons.

For my part, I believe that we do need publicly agreed criteria. Furthermore, we need them while many of these human fertility options still lie in the future. Without clearly established criteria we will be in danger of acting on instincts or prejudices in deciding to allow one form of fertility treatment and to disallow another. Certainly, as Christians we have strong reasons for wishing to see public criteria that protect new human life and that treat it with the uttermost seriousness and respect. For us human life is given to us by a loving God, it is created in the very image of God, and it is in the form of this life that God came to live among us.

The first criterion, I believe, is that we should not experiment with the lives of human beings without their informed consent unless we have the most serious of reasons for doing so. Babies obviously cannot give such consent, so we should not conduct experiments upon them unless for the most serious of reasons.

Some life-threatening genetic diseases may well constitute such a reason. One day it may be very tempting to seek to eliminate egregious genetic defects through germ-line surgery. But I doubt if a wish to have a baby, however deeply felt, is really a sufficient reason for human cloning. Such a wish may not even be an adequate reason for assisting the elderly to become parents.

A second criterion is that, if human life is treated with full seriousness and respect, we should use safe and tested methods first before attempting new and untried methods of fertility or germ-line surgery. The more we opt for extraordinary means, the less we will resort to the safer means we already possess. In many parts of the world it is still accepted that extended families should share the pleasure of their children with family members who cannot have their own. Even in Western societies many childless couples and single people use their parenting gifts for the benefit of others in society. And, in place of germ-line surgery, there are already programmes of genetic counselling for families at risk.[1]

A third criterion is that we should establish the risks of any potential treatment properly before it is ever used on human beings. This is exactly what happened 20 years ago with IVF. The techniques which enabled Louise Brown to be born had already been well tested in the agricultural world. Perhaps one day the risks of germ-line surgery will also be properly established so that it can be used safely on human beings. Yet it is difficult to foresee many agricultural uses for animal cloning, so it may be much harder properly to establish the prior risks involved in human cloning.

If these three criteria can be satisfied, then perhaps we should be less cautious. The Chief Rabbi is surely right in saying this week that humility is the first requirement in the use of godlike power. Yet if new techniques can genuinely reduce human suffering and promote health, but without an accompanying human risk, then it could be right to draw the present line differently. In the meantime we should not conduct such experiments on human life.

Spare embryos

2003

—————•◦•—————

Over the last week there have been four perplexing cases involving embryos:

1 *Frozen embryos.* Natallie Evans and Lorraine Hadley began a case in the High Court to allow them to have children using their frozen embryos. Both women are separated from former partners who have now withdrawn their consent for these embryos to be used. The 1990 Human Fertilisation and Embryology Act states that the consent of both parties is essential for embryos to be implanted.

2 *Fetal embryos.* Researchers from Israel and the Netherlands have taken tissue from the ovaries of aborted fetuses and grown them for a month in a laboratory. Because of a shortage of adult egg donors, this might pave the way for fetal eggs to be used one day within IVF treatment. However, after a public consultation, the British HFEA rejected such an option in 1994.

3 *Hermaphrodite embryos.* Researchers from Chicago have successfully transplanted clusters of cells taken from male embryos into three-day female embryos. Stating that they do not intend to produce adult hermaphrodites, they claim that the techniques developed might eventually help to correct defective genetic disorders in embryos before implantation.

4 *Saviour embryos.* The European Society of Human Reproduction and Embryology (ESHRE) judged that the HFEA had been wrong to turn down the Whitaker family but allow the Hashmi family to have pre-implantation genetic diagnosis (PGD) before IVF, in order to produce a so-called 'saviour sibling'. Members argued that the HFEA should have allowed both cases. The HFEA had argued that only the Hashmi case

had a clear benefit to the new child and that it was wrong to have PGD on an embryo solely for the benefit of an older sibling.

What on earth is the Christian to make of all of this? At face value it does seem that medical science is losing all respect for God's creation and treating human embryos as objects of mere curiosity. Paul Ramsey, [as already seen] an early critic of IVF and genetic manipulation, would have been exasperated. This seems exactly what he meant by labelling such activity as 'playing God'.

Yet many Christian couples who would otherwise have been childless have good reason to be grateful to the pioneers of IVF. There are also Christian families suffering from serious genetic disabilities who actively support genetic research on embryos. The world is not neatly divided between Christians who reject all of these techniques and non-Christians who accept them.

For Roman Catholics holding to current papal teaching, none of the four cases is allowable. All depend upon IVF, which itself is considered wrong because it severs the unitive and procreative functions of the sexual act (as, of course, does contraception). It also involves masturbation to collect the male semen.

For Christians who believe that full human life begins at conception, IVF is also wrong, unless every fertilized egg is implanted (as the women in the frozen embryos case want). Yet, because of the invasive nature of egg collection, IVF usually involves the fertilization of more eggs than are likely to be implanted. These spare fertilized eggs (embryos) are then frozen. However, British law requires frozen embryos to be destroyed if not used within five years.[1] Christians holding this position conclude that IVF results in the destruction of full human life.

This is not necessarily the end of the matter. In *Lost Icons* Archbishop Rowan Williams writes that, although considering abortion to be 'the termination of human life', he accepts that 'the termination of a pregnancy is not necessarily in all circumstances the worst possible moral option'.[2] His position counsels great caution on the part of Christians, but it might still allow at least some use of IVF.

The General Synod has just debated whether the use of embryos for stem-cell research into serious genetic conditions is ethical. Some members saw this research as wrong, some as morally desirable, and others were unsure. There is a need for continuing debate on this crucial issue within the Church, but it is frankly not easy to see how it will ever be resolved. We all might agree that moral seriousness and caution are needed, but we will still disagree about cases.

Furthermore, to engage meaningfully in debates in the public forum it is helpful to have common (and not simply Christian) criteria for rejecting particular developments in medical treatment or research: for example, whether there is properly informed consent; real benefit and a minimum of harm to the patients involved; no serious injustice to others.

Using these criteria, the first three cases at the beginning of this article can be disallowed. Frozen embryos are not the property of women alone, so the consent of both parties is needed.[3] Fetal embryos present a serious risk of harm since eggs are harvested from a fetus that itself has not been shown to be viable. Hermaphrodite embryo research is also premised upon a serious risk of harm: there are safer ways than genetic engineering of reducing genetic disability in at-risk families (notably using PGD).

The saviour embryos case is more difficult. The ESHRE decision does resolve a sense of injustice to the Whitakers. Yet the HFEA does have real scruples about 'designing' children solely for the benefit of others. However, the HFEA has been internally divided on the ethics of distinguishing between the families. After much soul searching, personally I would add the criterion of compassion to justice and allow PGD for both families.

Human reproductive cloning
2005

A major scientific breakthrough occurred this week. A team of medical scientists in Newcastle successfully cloned a human embryo, replicating research done earlier in South Korea.[1] Although the embryo died after five days the team has shown that the techniques which produced Dolly the sheep can also be applied to humans in order to produce therapeutic stem cells. It is even possible that one day someone with a serious degenerative disease, such as Parkinson's, will be cured by receiving cloned embryonic stem cells from his or her own body.

There is still a long way to go before therapy might be possible. The track record of gene therapy – once thought to be an imminent possibility but now proving difficult and dangerous – suggests that caution is needed at this stage of the research. This is a fascinating breakthrough, but there are many steps to go. The nucleus from an unfertilized egg has been successfully removed and replaced with the nucleus from an unrelated adult cell. After being treated chemically and given a mild electrical shock, it has been stimulated to divide as if it were a normal embryo. Much work is still needed to determine how to derive healthy stem cells from such a cloned embryo, how to preserve these stem cells without contaminating them, and finally how to use them safely and beneficially in human therapy.

The science involved is undoubtedly fascinating, but is it ethical? Many countries regard human reproductive cloning for whatever purpose as deeply repugnant and want it banned worldwide. Britain is still unusual for allowing embryonic (albeit highly regulated) stem-cell research. Opponents of human reproductive cloning, many of them religiously motivated, usually offer one of two broad criticisms, the first based upon a principled objection to human cloning and the second upon its consequences.

Julia Millington of the Pro-Life Alliance articulated the principled objection strongly this week in the *Daily Mail*: 'Cloning for research purposes, which involves the manufacture of human embryos destined for experimentation and subsequent destruction, is profoundly unethical. The deliberate destruction of human life at any stage of development has no place in a civilised society.' The neuroscientist Professor Neil Scolding of Bristol offered a milder version of the same argument in *The Guardian*: 'The ethical considerations cannot be brushed aside. You can argue about whether a cloned embryo is a person, but you cannot get away from the fact that it is alive and it is human.'

The milder version is probably too weak to carry much conviction. A vesicular mole [as noted earlier] is both alive and fertilized and human, but few would derive much moral status from that. However, the stronger version also faces difficulties about moral status. From a scientific perspective both cloned and uncloned IVF embryos could be implanted and might be able to gestate to term, but from a moral (and indeed legal) perspective cloned embryos should never be implanted. It is not simply that the Newcastle scientists do not intend to implant cloned embryos, but that it would be *intrinsically wrong* for them to do so. There are a few libertarian bioethicists, such as Professor Julian Savulescu of Oxford in *The Times Higher Education Supplement* this week, who argue that implanting would be ethical once the present dangers are overcome. However, there is an obvious flaw in their argument; the dangers can only be overcome by first experimenting upon human beings. I believe that attempts to clone human beings (i.e. reproductive cloning) are intrinsically wrong since it is always wrong to attempt risky interventions on human beings without their consent and with few if any obvious human benefits. Given this, there is surely something odd about according cloned 'embryos' moral or theological status as human embryos. Why not regard them instead as pieces of our own body that have been 'tricked' into behaving like embryos?

The second objection focuses upon the consequences of therapeutic cloning paving the way for reproductive cloning. Creating embryos by cell nuclear replacement is undoubtedly the first step in human reproductive cloning. [As seen earlier] the Donaldson Report,[2] which five years ago paved the way for this research in Britain, was well aware of this, but insisted that the regulatory powers of the HFEA (and now the Stem Cell Bank Steering Committee) were sufficient to ensure that cloned embryos are never developed beyond 14 days and are never implanted.

But the trouble is that even if such regulatory powers exist in Britain, they do not exist in all other countries. More than that, the knowledge gained in Britain about therapeutic cloning will be valuable elsewhere in the world to those determined to embark upon reproductive cloning. In an age of morally responsible science, it is no longer sufficient to say 'knowledge is knowledge' and wipe our hands of any responsibility for how this knowledge might be used by the less scrupulous.

Caution is needed as well as co-ordinated international action. There are serious dangers here both at a therapeutic level and in terms of global politics. But there is also the possibility of real benefit for vulnerable people, and for this reason I remain a cautious supporter of this research.

Part 4

DOCTORS AND PATIENTS

Priorities in healthcare
1997

———•◆•———

Perhaps the most difficult issue in medical ethics today is that of priorities. Given that medical resources are not infinite, what ethical criteria should be used to decide who is to be treated and who is not? On what ethical grounds are we to choose one treatment and not another? Or, to put it bluntly, how should we decide on one use of medical finances at the expense of another?

A recent case-study illustrates the hard decisions here. A local health council meeting was called to consider a proposal to relocate mental healthcare entirely into the district general hospital. The counterproposal was that a separate building – a rambling eighteenth-century house – should be used to relocate acute services from its present dilapidated buildings. An extra £200,000 annually would be needed for this counterproposal. The angry healthcare workers and patients present at the meeting argued that cost should not be the prime consideration. Patients with acute mental health problems are an extremely vulnerable group and should be given their own space, even if this costs more. The psychiatrists also argued that their work would be more difficult in the setting of a general hospital. They would be forced to refer more patients to a secure hospital some distance away. Quality of care must come before cost.

In the face of these arguments, the health service managers appeared to be uncaring and finance-driven. They argued that changes in surgical techniques, allied to the size of the local population, put the very existence of the general hospital, already in deficit, at risk. Without extra patients and services it might not survive at all. And since it was unlikely that new government funds could be found, the necessary £200,000 must be withdrawn from some other area of healthcare provision.

The meeting ended with a massive vote for the counterproposal. I was almost alone in voting for caution. For me the question of choosing one priority at the expense of another had never been properly addressed.

Healthcare is facing an enormous problem of its own 'success'. At least four factors are involved in this. The first is that healthcare technology costs are rising at twice the level of inflation. New powerful medical technology and drugs are often extremely expensive. Second, they enable more ill people to live longer. Indeed, in our generation we have seen, thank God, all sorts of people surviving from conditions that would surely have killed them in the past. Third, the elderly are being given more medical treatment, allowing them to live fuller and more active lives. And fourth, more medical conditions can be effectively treated. There is now a whole range of illnesses, once thought to be untreatable, which respond well to modern treatment.

Does Christian faith have anything to say about this? Two principles are particularly important, yet, as so often, they are in tension with each other. The first is the command to care especially for the vulnerable and needy (Matthew 25); the second is to be good stewards of our God-given resources. It was very encouraging to hear so many people committed to the first of these at the health council meeting. What I heard less about was the second.

Good stewardship is essential. It is not simply a question of finances, as the acute dilemmas facing organ transplant teams clearly show. In a recent inquiry, about a surgeon who refused to do a transplant on a 16-year-old girl who had damaged her liver taking Ecstasy, the issue of criteria for priorities was raised. It was suspected that the girl had not been treated because of her drug abuse. The surgeon argued that a national shortage of livers suitable for transplant surgery meant that she *had* to take difficult decisions about priorities. In this particular case she had decided about priorities on the grounds that a transplant was very unlikely to save the girl's life. Her youth might otherwise have given her medical priority over an elderly patient. However, non-effectiveness was the crucial criterion here for good stewardship. It was stressed in the inquiry that the culpability of the girl was not, and should not be, a relevant criterion.

Do we have to prioritize in a similar way when it comes to financial resources? One response to this question is simply 'no'. Instead of treating finances as a limited resource, we should rather increase expenditure on healthcare resources as a percentage of gross national product (GNP). Of course, increasing expenditure on the National Health Service (NHS), without raising taxes, entails spending less on other things – such as education, public amenities and the creation of new jobs. Even so, increasing public or private expenditure without any priorities may not be good stewardship which improves general health. After all, the USA spends 14 per cent of GNP and may not have better general health than the UK which spends 6 per cent of GNP.

Another option is to make more effective use of current re-sources. The new government has made this a major healthcare priority. Yet efficiency savings to achieve greater effectiveness are widely thought to take up too much of the working time of healthcare workers, to increase NHS bureaucracy and to reduce proper care to functional efficiency. Efficiency and effectiveness can too easily be confused. Nevertheless, inefficiency as such scarcely amounts to good stewardship.

It is difficult to escape the conclusion that healthcare provision does need to be prioritized. If some forms of treatment are to be regarded as priorities in the NHS (e.g. cancer, heart attacks and strokes, and indeed mental health), then others will probably become low priorities only offered privately (e.g. removing tattoos, reversing sterilization, and possibly most forms of IVF).

Perhaps the choice of particular buildings will assume a fairly low priority in this context. Yet how do we finally decide? The health council meeting was one attempt to find a democratic forum to resolve a difficult dilemma. Although it was well attended – encouragingly there were also several clergy present – it was inevitably focused, partisan and crisis-driven. Those with an axe to grind about mental healthcare dominated the proceedings.

Another proposal, which is currently being tested by the pres-tigious King's Fund, is to set up local review panels which can take a cooler and more strategic overview. Yet another proposal is to have regular questionnaire surveys of public opinion. They tend to find that most people give priority to the young and the acutely ill. Yet their weakness is illustrated by an intricate survey reported in a recent *British Medical Journal* article which made no mention of hospital casualty services at all.[1]

Of course, the issue of priorities in medicine will never be finally resolved. This is an issue which should indeed be given sustained and ongoing attention by the public. Yet within this there is a real need for a distinctive Christian voice – keeping alive a concern both for the vulnerable *and* for good stewardship.

Organ donation

2000

———————•◦•———————

This week the BMA published a new report, *Organ Donation in the 21st Century: Time for a Consolidated Approach*. I must declare an interest, since I was a member of the working group that shaped it. But from this I know how thorough the BMA is and just how widely it consults. This is an important issue and the report offers an up-to-date moral and practical guide. Churches are inevitably involved, not least because a surprising number of clergy and lay people have themselves had a kidney, heart, lung or liver transplant. Many more will also be waiting anxiously to see whether they or someone they love can have an organ transplant. And parish priests will know at first hand just how distressing this can be.

The main problem can be stated quite simply. During the 1990s there has been a decline in organ transplants in the United Kingdom but an increase in those on the active national waiting list. So much so that there are currently over five thousand people on this active list and possibly another six thousand who could be added to it. Partly as a result of safer roads in this country, there is now a considerable shortage of suitable organs available for transplants, yet, with dramatic advances in transplantation surgery and after-care, many more people could benefit from them. Need and availability are increasingly out of phase.[1]

How is this problem to be addressed in a way that is thoroughly ethical? This is the question that the BMA seeks to answer. Throughout, it attempts to balance the requirements of justice, consent and care for the vulnerable. In the wake of the shocking reports of hospitals not getting the consent of parents to retain organs for research from their dead children, the BMA report treads cautiously. It is also aware that there are all sorts of interdictions and sensitivities surrounding public attitudes to dead bodies. There are also paradoxes. Not the least of these is that 70 per cent of people interviewed say that they would be willing to donate their organs, yet only 20 per cent of us actually carry a donor card. We are a curious lot.

Of course, there may come a time when organ donation from human beings is no longer necessary. It might one day be possible to develop effective and reliable mechanical hearts. Or it might be possible to transplant animal organs (xenotransplants) which are not rejected by humans and which do not carry a risk of animal diseases affecting humans. It might even be possible to use cell nuclear replacement technology to develop comparable tissue for transplantation (therapeutic cloning). However, in the meantime there remains a very serious medical and pastoral need for more human organs for donation.

This situation could be helped by improving the co-ordination, infrastructure and training within transplant services. The BMA report estimates that currently two-thirds of suitable organs are not donated. It argues that the 'consolidated approach' highlighted in its subtitle is essential and that a greater awareness of the need for more organ donations across medical and voluntary sectors is required. In some countries, such as Spain, this has resulted recently in a considerable improvement. There could also be a much more concerted attempt to publicize donor cards and to make registration on the donor register easier. By linking donor registration to driving licence applications and to new registrations with GPs, there is already evidence that more of us can be encouraged to be potential donors. In the case of kidney donation there has also been an increasing number of live donors – often parents giving one of their kidneys to their child. Such live donations now represent one in six kidney transplants and are surely one of the most striking examples of altruism in society today. There is still a need for caution here, and the report rightly insists upon a number of strict conditions: the risk to the donor must be low; the donor must be fully informed; the decision to donate must be entirely voluntary and not due to coercion or the offer of an inducement; and the transplant procedure must have a good chance of providing a successful outcome for the recipient.

Yet the BMA report argues that all of these steps are still insufficient. It is at this point that it becomes more controversial and clashes with the position taken consistently by the Department of Health (DoH).[2] It argues for a move from 'opt in' (the DoH position) to 'opt out' or, more accurately, to a position of 'presumed consent with safeguards'. The report argues that since most people do still wish to act in an altruistic manner and are sympathetic to organ donation (even if they are lax about carrying donor cards), then there are good reasons for presuming consent and requiring the small number of those who object to donation to register their views. In effect, donation would become the default position. Close relatives would not be asked to give permission for the organs of their dead relative to be used for donation. Instead, they would be informed that the individual had not registered an objection to donation while alive and, unless they objected – either because they were aware of an unregistered objection by the individual or because it would cause a close relative or long-term partner major distress – the donation would proceed. So there is a clear safeguard for those closest to the dead person, but the expectation is that most of us would wish our organs to be donated to benefit others if at all possible.

Will this proposal work? Some doubt whether it will increase transplants. The statistics here are difficult, but the BMA report does put up a strong case. Others, including perhaps the government, fear accusations about the 'nanny state' and the loss of individual liberty if registered objections are inadvertently overlooked. The BMA's response is that care must be taken to make sure that this does not happen, but that finally patient needs require a bolder approach than the present one. Too many lives are currently being lost of people who could have benefited from a transplant if an organ had been available. Most of us would wish to help them if we possibly could. Thank God, we are still surprisingly altruistic.

So what can you do? Carry a donor card. Definitely. I believe that we should also press for the BMA position of presumed consent with safeguards and encourage our politicians to be bolder. For me this is not an expression of the nanny state but rather of corporate altruism. The Church could properly play a greater part in helping to promote such altruism.

Organ donation at Christmas

2001

———•◦•———

One unusual, but very practical, gift this Christmas could be the offer of organ donation. Of course, this could be the expensive, musical variety of organ donation . . . no doubt very welcome in some churches. More realistically, for most of us it would simply entail joining the organ donor register. It costs people almost nothing but it could improve the quality of life of someone else or even save a person's life.

Last year I wrote[1] about the then newly published BMA report *Organ Donation in the 21st Century*. It highlighted the fact that more lives could be saved and the quality of life improved for many if more organs were available for transplants. There were then over 5,000 people on the active waiting list for a transplant. A year later some 5,500 people are waiting for a transplant. The gap between supply and demand grows year on year. Developments in transplant surgery are increasingly hampered by a lack of donated organs. The UK now has one of the lowest donor rates in Europe and there are actually fewer transplant operations today than there were ten years ago.

In the wake of their report, the BMA, together with the Royal Colleges and charities such as the British Kidney Patient Association, have set up a Transplant Partnership. This Partnership has just launched a major Christmas campaign aimed at raising awareness of the organ donor register, getting people to sign up to the register and calling for improvements to the organ donation system in the UK. The Transplant Partnership is very keen that churches should be a part of this Christmas campaign.

The Partnership has also commissioned a new opinion survey that highlights the gap between what people do and what they intend to do. Unfortunately churchgoers are little different from the rest of the population on organ donation. Only a small number of us have signed up to the organ donor register, yet when asked most say that in general terms they support donation. Only 3 per cent of churchgoers and non-churchgoers alike in a recent survey reply that they do not agree with organ donation at all and 8 per cent that they would not join the organ donation register. Two out of five people say that they have never heard of this register, but half of these add that they would sign up to it if they knew how. In short, many of us (churchgoers included) are in favour of donation but have made little or no effort to become potential organ donors ourselves.

In reality it is not difficult to sign up to the register. There is both a telephone line (0300 123 23 23) and a website (<www.uktransplant.org.uk>) available for new potential donors. People changing GPs should also receive a form enabling them to register. By joining the register people make their intentions clear. Indeed, the most common reason why relatives refuse permission for donation is that they do not know the deceased's prior wishes. Yet many relatives, given time and space for reflection, later regret refusing.

As Christians we have several strong reasons for taking this practical step. A concern for the vulnerable lay at the very heart of Jesus' ministry. Again and again he even broke the Sabbath to heal those in need and criticized others for putting scruples before human compassion. In their healing ministry today doctors, surgeons and nurses are constantly mentioned in our intercessions. For most of us their skills are now an essential part of God's work in the world. And, above all, the new life of the baby at Bethlehem reminds us that giving is truly God's work.

Seductive evil

2002

———•◆•———

Within a week we have seen judicial verdicts delivered on two astonishingly evil men. First there was Dame Janet Smith's interim report concluding that Dr Harold Shipman murdered at least 215 of his patients. And then there was the conviction at the Old Bailey of Nicholas van Hoogstraten who, after years of brutal intimidation, was found guilty of hiring two assassins to murder a business associate.

How is the Christian to understand such evil?

Secular accounts of Shipman have tended to talk about his arrogance and wish to control other people. Some have mentioned trauma after the death of his mother and others his isolation and fantasy world. Like Jo Ind (*Church Times*, 26 July) I don't find any of these explanations particularly helpful. There are plenty of arrogant control-freaks, as well as those who have suffered deep trauma or live in a fantasy world, but they don't become mass murderers. So why did Shipman?

There may be a more credible explanation hinted at in the accounts of Hoogstraten. In one of his earlier trials it was mentioned that he saw himself as 'an emissary of Beelzebub'. Apparently he was fascinated as a young man by Graham Greene's *Brighton Rock* and perversely identified with its villain, Pinkie Brown. Yet despite a number of newspapers noting these two features, I didn't see any offering an explicitly religious explanation of why he acted as he did.

In a remarkable recent book, *Evil and Christian Ethics*,[1] Gordon Graham does offer such an explanation. He writes as a professional philosopher (he is Professor of Philosophy at Aberdeen University) who also has profound theological interests (he is a non-stipendiary priest in the Scottish Episcopal Church). He argues at length that secular accounts of evil are inadequate. They either seek to explain away evil as some disorder or malfunction, or they maintain that there is no such thing as objective evil. They also, so he argues, tend to offer no hope beyond evil. In contrast, he presents a powerful case for thinking that a Christian narrative can provide a more adequate basis for understanding and over-coming evil and that to believe coherently in the existence of objective evil requires us to believe in a providential God.

Now, of course, such claims will immediately be greeted with much scepticism in the secular world, since it is widely assumed that the problem of evil presents theists with a unique and insurmountable difficulty. Gordon Graham is well aware of this and offers an extended account of this 'problem', arguing in the process that secularists actually have a greater problem of evil (to put it bluntly, if the world is considered by them to be so evil why do they stay alive?). After a disturbing account of earlier serial killers, he concludes that 'humanism cannot explain (so to speak) the evil of evil, and naturalistic science, even of a well-informed psychological kind, cannot explain its occurrence'.

In contrast, he argues that a strong feature of biblical under-standings of evil is that it is deeply seductive. Indeed, the very fact that we find accounts of Shipman and Hoogstraten so fascinating (as well as repulsive) is a good indication of this seductiveness. Whether it is the serpent in Genesis 3 or the devil in the wilder-ness in Matthew 4 and Luke 4, evil is seen in the Bible as being deeply seductive. And finally it takes the Son of God wholly to resist such seductive evil.

Of course, Christians remain deeply divided about the status of this evil. Gordon Graham believes in a personal devil of some form, whereas other theologians (myself included) do not. Frankly it makes very little difference for a Christian, since any form of evil (whether a personal devil or an impersonal but still deeply seductive evil) is finally and mysteriously a part of God's creation. Christianity has long since rejected Manichaeism with its vision of primeval conflict between the equal forces of good and evil.

Hoogstraten was apparently fascinated with evil from childhood. He received his first criminal conviction when he was 11 and delighted in swindling fellow pupils at his Roman Catholic school out of their valuable stamps. Perhaps it was no accident that he saw himself as 'an emissary of Beelzebub' and those closest to him not as friends but as his 'lieutenants'.

But what about Shipman? Fewer personal details of this intensely secretive man are publicly available (Gordon Graham, in contrast, was able to use detailed accounts of interviews made with several US serial killers). However, there is the track record of Shipman's murders. The first of these, in 1975, might have appeared to him as an act of mercy-killing on a terminally ill patient or even as physician-assisted suicide. For nine years his victims were all very elderly. But then the pattern began to change. Patients as young as 41 started to be murdered. And then there were neighbours who were murdered apparently to protect Shipman himself from disclosure. After 20 years the rate of his murders increased hugely, and then his final victim was apparently plain murder for financial gain.

By using the theological language of seductive evil and its accompaniment, human sin, we might be able to understand these two evil men more clearly. Gordon Graham (and indeed Alistair McFadyen in his important book *Bound to Sin?*[2]) helps us to do this. Because evil is seductive it is also progressive, even incremental, and repeated sinful behaviour weakens our capacity to resist such evil. Wisdom in the Apocrypha combines these ideas, reminding us both about our 'fascination with wickedness' and that wickedness in turn 'blinds' us.

Even Shipman's drug addiction – so readily identified in many secular accounts simply as an illness or even as a genetic disposition – may be seen, at least in part, in terms of seductive evil and repeated sinful behaviour. One influential school within addiction studies suggests that the addict typically crosses a series of thresholds. For example, before an alcoholic typically reaches the stage of physical dependence upon alcohol and is unable to stop without considerable pain and trauma, he or she has crossed from social drinking to secretive drinking, from evening drinking to morning drinking, from drinking to enhance life to a life organized in order to drink, and so forth.[3]

Just as we all have the capacity to be fascinated by evil, so we also know that a second sinful act is easier to commit than the first.

Few of us, thank God, succumb to monstrous evil. Yet we can see that the early steps of such evil are present within each of us.

Step by step, both Shipman and Hoogstraten did gradually succumb to monstrous evil. Seductive evil – present in all people except Jesus – overwhelmed them. In Shipman's case, the Christian virtues of compassion, care and trust seemed to become distorted means of hiding deeply wicked actions. Or perhaps to the end he really was a compassionate and caring doctor to most of his patients (as many of them insisted before his trial). If he were alive today, Lord Longford would surely have insisted that both men are still redeemable. That is very important. Yet, if Gordon Graham is right, it is also important to be more frank about evil.

Consent

2003

———•◆•———

The High Court judgment last week that two women cannot have their frozen embryos implanted without the men's consent has clarified medical law. Consent of both parties was judged to be essential and not to be overruled by appeals to the Human Rights Act. But was the judgment ethical? And how should Christians respond? After all, unless a successful appeal is made,[1] apparently healthy embryos will be destroyed and one of the two women will remain childless.

Over the last generation, the primacy of consent has gradually become established in medical ethics and law. In the past many doctors believed that it was their role alone to decide what treatment to give a patient. It was they who were medically qualified and in a position to know what was in their patients' best interests. Patients were not to be burdened by medical decisions that they scarcely understood. Benevolent paternalism was often regarded as good medicine.

Not today and certainly not after the Ms B case[2] – the very severely disabled woman who successfully argued two years ago that she should be allowed to come off a life-support machine. The judge interviewed Ms B at length (interestingly, both were practising Christians) solely to ascertain whether or not she was competent to make this decision and had understood the situation and available options. Once the judge had decided that she was competent, adequately informed and not under duress, she ruled that Ms B's decision to come off the life-support machine (and, as a result, die) must be respected. It was not for the Hospital Trust (or for Christians opposed to this decision) to decide otherwise.

Consent or choice by competent patients not to have medical treatment, or for parts of one's body (or that of one's child) not

84

to be used in medical research, is now binding. After several national scandals and two public enquiries, it is now clear that doctors cannot normally retain organs or body parts without explicit consent from patients or their immediate relatives (unless, of course, crime is involved). Even when it is in the interests of a patient to receive some treatment, this cannot overrule the explicit wishes of a competent patient. And even when it is in the interests of medical research, consent must now be given to retain patient body parts.

The Department of Health's very recent document *Confidentiality: NHS Code of Practice*[3] extends this to information about patients. It insists that healthcare staff need to inform patients carefully when information might be shared by others in the healthcare system in order to provide them with proper care. Staff are now expected to check that information on disclosure has been read and understood by patients and that they have been given the option of deciding against disclosure (even if this reduces the effectiveness of their treatment).

Properly informed patient consent now involves at least the following:

- sufficient and understandable information about a particular medical intervention that enables competent patients to make an informed choice
- time to reach a settled and non-coerced choice
- proper awareness of other options (including non-treatment)
- respect for a decision once reached
- an option for patients to change their minds before the medical intervention is actually made.

Some theologians have argued that this current emphasis upon consent is a sign of the Fall, making a sinful idol of the self. They argue that it reflects a misguided notion of individual autonomy, itself a product of the secular Enlightenment.

In contrast, I regard a respect for properly informed patient consent as a sign of moral maturity and of treating people as people. For me, it is also an expression of a mature theology. The incarnate God comes to us in self-imposed humility (Phil. 2.6–8), bidding but not coercing us to follow (Mark 1.16–19). Indeed, it seems that God deliberately created a world in which we even have a choice to be evil, knowing that only in such a world can there also be a real possibility of moral goodness.[4] If God so chooses to act only with our consent, how much more should we respect the consent of others?

However, there is a need to make a careful distinction between, on the one hand, consent to have or not to have treatment, and a conviction, on the other, that an individual has a right to have whatever treatment he or she likes regardless of other people. It is probably the latter that theologians who attack autonomy have in mind. I doubt if they themselves would want doctors to give them medical treatment without proper explanation or choice or to use their abandoned body parts in research they regarded as obnoxious.

The women who wished to have their frozen embryos implanted without the men's consent were in danger of voicing this latter conviction. Apparently they regarded it as their right to use the embryos regardless of the strong and settled wishes of the men. Yet they knew at the outset that consent was needed by both parties since each had contributed to the embryos.

Very sadly, one of the women will now be unable to have children using her own ova. Yet it would have run a coach, horses and motor cavalcade through hard-won moral and legal gains about consent if the women had won their case.

Impurity, sin and disease
2003

AIDS evokes powerful and disturbing connections between impurity, sin and disease. Christianity simultaneously carries these connections and challenges them.

The story of the healing of the paralytic man in the first three Gospels does seem to make connections at least between sin and disease. Jesus' opening words to the man are 'Son, your sins are forgiven' (Mark 2.5). Even when challenged by the scribes present, he persists in talking about sins in this healing context.

On this interpretation, Jesus stood in a long Jewish tradition linking disease and disaster with personal sin. This tradition is particularly evident in Job and in a number of the Psalms. It is God 'who forgives all your iniquity, who heals all your diseases' (Ps. 103.3). This link also leads to some confusion. Both Job and the Psalmists puzzle at times about why the wicked can actually prosper. Yet this is only a puzzle in a context that presumes that sin normally leads to disaster and disease.

The links continued in medieval attitudes towards those seen today as having learning disabilities and psychiatric illnesses. The long history of witch hunts and persecution that scarred Christian Europe, together with the treatment of 'demoniacs' and lepers, owed much to these links. And to the present day they continue in attitudes towards those contracting sexually transmitted diseases. The identification of HIV & AIDS as 'God's punishment' is part of a long tradition.

Mary Douglas's classic 1966 study *Purity and Danger*[1] helps us to understand the links made in this tradition. Although some of the details of this extraordinary and provocative book are now contested (even by herself), its overall vision has transformed attitudes to impurity, sin and disease. Writing as an anthropologist (who is also a practising Roman Catholic)[2] she argued that notions of purity and impurity are ubiquitous, but also varied and complex. The varying ways that we clean our houses today (partly for hygiene but also for order and comfort) indicate that complex notions of purity and impurity do not simply belong to ancient or tribal worlds.

She suggested that notions of impurity become particularly powerful (and dangerous) when they coincide with moral notions. Taking the example of tramps allowed to sleep in the vicinity of churches, she argued that purity lines could be broken when they choose to sleep instead on the church benches. If tramps are then thought to endanger other people, moral as well as purity lines are broken. In addition, many notions of purity involve sexuality, often (but not always) with men seeking to control women. Menstrual blood is especially linked with impurity in many cultures.

Lines that intersect purity, morality and sexuality signal serious danger. The recent Anglican debate about homosexuality provides an obvious example. The strong passions generated within this debate do seem to indicate that deep-seated notions, owing much to traditional ideas about impurity and danger (themselves varying from one culture to another), are involved. Perhaps that is why they are so difficult to resolve peaceably. Reactions to HIV & AIDS are another example.

Alongside this tradition in Christian history – linking impurity, sin and disease – is another that challenges it. Arguably it is a tradition with rather stronger claims to represent Jesus as portrayed in the first three Gospels.

According to this tradition, Jesus deliberately challenges the prevalent attitudes to purity. In the early chapters of Mark, Jesus repeatedly breaks the Sabbath in the interests of the vulnerable. In the Gospels at large he touches the 'impure' lepers and those with severe disabilities and, in turn, is touched by the woman rendered 'impure' by heavy menstrual bleeding. And a simplistic connection between sin and disease or disaster is questioned (Luke 13.1–5 and John 9.2).

This tradition has also played an important part in Christian history. Mary Douglas provided a startling and somewhat shocking example:

St Catherine of Sienna, when she felt revulsion from the wounds she was tending, is said to have bitterly reproached herself. Sound hygiene was incompatible with charity, so she deliberately drank of a bowl of pus.

The nineteenth-century Anglican social reformer Josephine Butler provides another example. Despite being married to an Anglican priest, who was both a headmaster and a cathedral canon, she worked tirelessly among prostitutes and campaigned successfully on their behalf against the naval Contagious Diseases Acts. She crossed so many of Mary Douglas's lines that it took the Church of England a century to recognize publicly the importance and courage of her work.

A further example comes from modern India. Although Christians in much of India form only a small minority of the population, they are disproportionately represented in nursing. Unlike their Hindu compatriots, Christians are less likely to believe that nursing involves them in impurity through contact with the sick and diseased.

Within this second Christian tradition a separation tends to be made between impurity, sin and disease. Doctors are not to moralize about the past behaviour of their patients. Even when sexual promiscuity does characterize some (but certainly not all) of those who contract HIV, this does not affect the medical treatment and care they are given. Similarly, the smoker who develops lung cancer and the alcoholic requiring a liver transplant are both to be treated simply as vulnerable patients in need of help.

Of course, there are still points of danger. The alcoholic who has a liver transplant but then resumes drinking is likely to become an object of public hostility. Similarly the carrier of HIV, who knowingly risks infecting others through unprotected sexual intercourse, tends to evoke strong moral panic. Most dangerous of all, in recent perceptions, is the paedophile who has served time in prison but is now released into the community.

Society does need to be protected. The contagious and the disturbed can be a danger to others even if they act unintentionally. However, we also need to be protected from those making connections, without careful thought, between impurity, sin and disease.

Trust in doctors

2005

———•◆•———

Recently two judicial cases, a government public consultation and a debate in the House of Lords, have raised serious questions about the changing relationship between doctors and their patients. The comfortable but often paternalistic Dr Finlays of the past are being replaced by healthcare teams, group practices, out-of-hours services and NHS Direct. Trust in your own personal and confidential doctor appears seriously diminished. And patients, in turn, now seem to be consumers – requiring impersonal healthcare professionals to deliver services and treatments that they demand.

Of course, this change can easily be exaggerated, but it has been seriously tested in the last three months.

In July the Court of Appeal considered the case of Oliver Leslie Burke, who suffers from a severe neurological condition that may eventually leave him incapacitated. Mr Burke won a judgment a year ago to the effect that he should still be given artificial nutrition and hydration when incapacitated, whatever the doctors involved thought. It was argued then that under the European Convention on Human Rights patients in his position did have a right to require treatment. However, the Court of Appeal overturned this judgment, arguing that patients do not have such a right.[1]

In October Mr Justice Hedley reconsidered his earlier judgment about baby Charlotte Wyatt, who has serious brain damage. Her parents, both committed Roman Catholics, were appealing against his original judgment that doctors would not be breaking the law if they refused to revive Charlotte if she stopped breathing. The judge now concluded that:

The consultant does not take orders from the family any more than he gives them. He acts in what he sees as the best interests of the child. In so doing, however, parental wishes should be accommodated as far as professional judgment and conscience will permit, but no further.

It may seem odd that either of these cases came to court in the first place. Good communication between doctors and patients would normally prevent such judicial confrontation. And would doctors really refuse to treat either Mr Burke despite his known wishes or baby Charlotte despite pleas from her distraught parents? It may be a sign of what Baroness Onora O'Neill terms 'a culture of suspicion' in her influential Reith and Gifford Lectures.[2] Perhaps we no longer trust professionals (including doctors) to act compassionately.

Yet both cases did come to court and many in medical ethics feared that, if the final judgments had been different, doctors in future would simply be required to accede to patient demands whatever their clinical judgment. So patients, demanding, say, antibiotics for viral infections or caesareans on social grounds, would have the final say. Patient autonomy would be determinative.

This last point was central in October to the bishops' successful resistance in the House of Lords to legalizing voluntary euthanasia. In the debate on the *Assisted Dying* report[3] they argued repeatedly that if patient autonomy were to be finally determinative in this area then culture and law would be seriously damaged, affecting other vulnerable patients and the doctor–patient relationship itself. It now seems likely that Lord Joffe will drop his attempt to legalize voluntary euthanasia and focus instead upon assisted suicide. This may be more difficult for the bishops to resist, especially if Lord Joffe removes doctors from the legal process of assisted suicide. After all, even if (following Augustine) the bishops consider suicide itself (let alone assisting suicide) to be sinful, few of them may wish to see it criminalized as it was before 1961. Lord Joffe will undoubtedly argue that it is one thing for Christians to believe that assisted suicide is sinful but quite another to believe that it should remain criminalized.[4]

Finally the government's Public Consultation Review of the Human Fertilisation and Embryology Act[5] is currently asking important questions about patient autonomy and the proper role of doctors in fertility treatment. Just before the general election the Science and Technology Select Committee presented a libertarian (but by no means unanimous) report that was highly critical of the HFEA and wished to deregulate most forms of fertility treatment. The government resisted much of this but is still asking searching questions about the 'need for a father' in fertility treatment,[6] about the welfare of children born from such treatment and about who might be able to access knowledge about donor parents. Doctors often feel in the firing line in this area (many hate to discriminate) and patients, in turn, can be very demanding.

Can theologians easily resolve these dilemmas? I doubt if we can. Simply condemning 'patient autonomy' is manifestly naive. Few of us really wish to return to the paternalism of the past. We do expect doctors to involve us fully in clinical choices that affect ourselves. Nevertheless, we have good biblical grounds for still believing that 'trust', and especially mutual trust, is important. Trust or faith [as seen earlier] is a crucial and dominant feature of the Synoptic healing stories. It is also multi-layered. Three different levels of trust or faith can be seen in these stories. The first is faithful trust in Jesus as healer (demonstrated either by the persistent words or by the determined actions either of those who would be healed or of their family or friends). The second is trust or faith as a mutual relationship between Jesus and those to be healed or their family or friends. And the third is faith or trust as a response to God.

Set in this wider context, good healing does involve mutual trust and the autonomy of both the healer and the one to be healed. For believers it is our trust in God that finally grounds this mutual relationship between doctor and patient. We may not share this final level of trust with all others in a pluralist society, but we can and should be champions of mutual trust.

Jesus, community compassion and HIV prevention

2007

——————•◆•——————

In what ways might values from the Gospel healing stories contribute to HIV prevention today?[1]

Consider, for example, this story recounted in the first chapter of Mark:

> A leper came to him begging him, and kneeling he said to him, 'If you choose, you can make me clean.' Moved with pity, Jesus stretched out his hand and touched him, and said to him, 'I do choose. Be made clean!' Immediately the leprosy left him, and he was made clean. After sternly warning him he sent him away at once, saying to him, 'See that you say nothing to anyone; but go, show yourself to the priest, and offer for your cleansing what Moses commanded, as a testimony to them.' But he went out and began to proclaim it freely, and to spread the word, so that Jesus could no longer go into a town openly, but stayed out in the country; and people came to him from every quarter. (Mark 1.40–45)

It was a 'leper' who came to Jesus. Except, of course, he almost certainly was not a 'leper' in any medical sense. *Sara'at* in the Jewish Bible or *lepra* in the New Testament are not simply to be identified with the bacterial infection Hansen's disease, or *Elephantiasis graecorum* (which is how leprosy would be identified today).[2] None of the crucial features of Hansen's disease (anaesthetic areas of the skin, painless and progressive ulceration of the extremities, and facial nodules) are ever mentioned in the Bible.[3] Rather, the person who came to Jesus had already been stigmatized by his community as being a 'leper', as someone who should be segregated from the community as being profoundly 'impure'.

This 'leper' came to Jesus 'begging' him and (according to some texts) 'kneeling'. Jesus in response was 'moved with pity/compassion' (some texts have 'anger'). Compassion [as seen earlier] is not just empathy, placing yourself in the position of another, but identifying someone in real need, 'suffering alongside' him or her and being determined to help if you possibly can. Compassion is both passionate and focused upon help. Then Jesus 'stretched out his hand and touched' the 'leper', showing astonishing disregard for the impurity consequences involved.[4] In this he was quite unlike Elisha, who stayed in his house, kept a distance from Naaman the 'leper' outside and gave his command through a messenger.[5] Compassionate care indeed!

In the parallel healing story of the ten lepers, told only in Luke, Jesus used a phrase repeated in other healing stories: 'your faith has made you well' (Luke 17.19). If compassion and care occur frequently in healing stories then so does faith . . . sometimes in the sense of 'trust' (particularly trust that Jesus can indeed heal) and other times nearer to 'belief'; and usually the faith of the person to be healed but occasionally the faith of others. Faith in some sense can even be a requirement of healing or, at least, its absence can be an explanation of why healing was not possible (Mark 6.6).

Characteristically, the story of the single 'leper' also involves restraint and humility, or rather a lack of restraint on the part of the one who was healed. Jesus sternly warned him, as he warned others:

> 'See that you say nothing to anyone' . . . but he went out and began to proclaim it freely, and to spread the word, so that Jesus could no longer go into a town openly.

Compassion, care, faith and humility run deeply through the healing stories and have much to teach us about good healthcare.[6] In addition, like many others, I have come to see strong affinities between the way 'lepers' in the Bible were stigmatized by their local community, but emphatically not by Jesus, and the way that those living with HIV are too often stigmatized today. Of course Hansen's disease and HIV are medically quite different from each other. But at the level of community misperceptions and stigmatization they have much in common. The followers of Jesus manifestly must respond to people living with HIV as Jesus responded to those perceived to be 'lepers' . . . that is, with compassion, care, faith and humility.

Community compassion versus community cohesion

All of this I simply assume here. But there is more to be discovered in this story from Mark about *community* compassion. This is, after all, a story that exemplifies a central tension within contextual theology. In it, the norms of the local community are simultaneously both challenged and affirmed. The complex requirements of Jewish purity laws are both broken and sustained in a single story. For those biblical scholars who see Jesus as one who overturns Jewish laws, the touching of the impure 'leper' confirms a pattern displayed in Jesus' table fellowship with sinners, breaking the Sabbath and being touched by the woman made impure from menstrual blood. However, for those who see Jesus as a generally observant Jew there is his command to 'show yourself to the priest, and offer for your cleansing what Moses commanded' as is required in Leviticus 13 and 14. Confusingly, the story can be read either way.[7]

My own suggestion is to see this as a story that upholds community norms when they do not conflict with the demands of compassion, that is to say the demands of the kingdom of God, but to challenge them when they do. Such compassion even takes precedence over strongly held and principled scruples. So Jesus upholds the formal requirements of Leviticus 13 and 14, yet as a healer 'moved with pity, Jesus stretched out his hand and touched' the 'leper'. The formal requirements of the local community were sustained but the personal practice was quite different.

This pattern is shown even more clearly in the following story, this time from Luke:

> Now he was teaching in one of the synagogues on the sabbath. And just then there appeared a woman with a spirit that had crippled her for eighteen years. She was bent over and was quite unable to stand up straight. When Jesus saw her, he called her over and said, 'Woman, you are set free from your ailment.' When he laid his hands on her, immediately she stood up straight and began praising God. But the leader of the synagogue, indignant because Jesus had cured on the sabbath, kept saying to the crowd, 'There are six days on which work ought to be done; come on those days and be cured, and not on the sabbath day.' But the Lord answered him and said,

'You hypocrites! Does not each of you on the sabbath untie his ox or his donkey from the manger, and lead it away to give it water? And ought not this woman, a daughter of Abraham whom Satan bound for eighteen long years, be set free from this bondage on the sabbath day?' When he said this, all his opponents were put to shame; and the entire crowd was rejoicing at all the wonderful things that he was doing. (Luke 13.10–17)

Viewed from the synagogue community's perspective, its leader was obviously correct: 'There are six days on which work ought to be done; come on those days and be cured, and not on the sabbath day.' The woman had been crippled for 18 years. One more day after all those years would have mattered little in the interests of keeping communal norms about the Sabbath. Jesus' response [as noted earlier] was astonishingly sharp: 'You hypocrites!'

In the Synoptic Gospels the charge of hypocrisy is always made by Jesus (13 times in Matthew) and is characteristically levelled at the religiously observant and their leaders. In this story the religious leader and his congregation are denounced as hypocrites, as 'actors' who say one thing but do another.[8] Or, to express this in terms of pastoral theology, they break the relationship between faith and practice. They claim the high ground of religious faith but in the process ignore the accompanying requirements of compassionate practice.

Compassion, truth and shame

In the context of HIV, hypocrisy by community leaders has been only too evident. Perhaps it is the hypocrisy of leaders hiding information about prevalence, denying the link between HIV and AIDS, or claiming that HIV only affects the gay community. Or perhaps, and most shocking among religious leaders, it is the denial that their own community and pastors are themselves living with HIV. Communal fidelity and truth-telling are key components in HIV prevention, yet the record of churches has all too often been riddled with hypocrisy.

If Jesus responded to the vulnerable with compassion, care, faith and humility, he responded to those religious people who ignored their plight with a sharp denunciation of hypocrisy. And 'when he said this, all his opponents were put to shame'.

The issue of 'shame' is especially sensitive in the context of HIV. 'Stigmatization' and 'shame' are closely connected, but they are not always identical. People have a deplorable tendency to stigmatize others, but they can properly feel shame about this tendency and thus about their own behaviour. All too often communities, even church communities, have seen fit to stigmatize those living with HIV. Stigmatizing (and even shaming) people who cannot undo their condition is particularly cruel and deeply harmful. Those with disabilities have all too often been stigmatized in this way. The history of 'leprosy' demonstrates this all too clearly. Emphatically, Jesus did not do that to the woman in this story. Yet he did 'put to shame' the community that had failed to show her compassion.

Perhaps communities that stigmatize those living with HIV, or that condone predatory male sexual behaviour that helps to spread HIV, can appropriately be shamed. This does appear to be possible in the third story:

> Early in the morning he came again to the temple. All the people came to him and he sat down and began to teach them. The scribes and the Pharisees brought a woman who had been caught in adultery; and making her stand before all of them, they said to him, 'Teacher, this woman was caught in the very act of committing adultery. Now in the law Moses commanded us to stone such women. Now what do you say?' They said this to test him, so that they might have some charge to bring against him. Jesus bent down and wrote with his finger on the ground. When they kept on questioning him, he straightened up and said to them, 'Let anyone among you who is without sin be the first to throw a stone at her.' And once again he bent down and wrote on the ground. When they heard it, they went away, one by one, beginning with the elders; and Jesus was left alone with the woman standing before him. Jesus straightened up and said to her, 'Woman, where are they? Has no one condemned you?' She said, 'No one, sir.' And Jesus said, 'Neither do I condemn you. Go your way, and from now on do not sin again.'   (John 8.2–11)

It is generally recognized that this is indeed an ancient story about Jesus but that it did not originally form a part of the Fourth

Gospel.[9] In the context of understanding compassion it is particularly important, although it requires sensitive interpretation.

Once again it is the religiously observant who take the moral high ground but are finally put to shame by Jesus. This time they are not defending the Sabbath. They have found a woman who has apparently flouted sexual norms: 'Teacher, this woman was caught in the very act of committing adultery.' As in many religious communities today, it is sexual activity that is identified as being especially sinful.

In the story Jesus does not deny the role of sin. The woman herself is finally told 'from now on do not sin again'; whatever she has done is not condoned. Yet she is explicitly not condemned by Jesus and everyone else is reminded that they are not 'without sin'. She is not stigmatized as an 'adulterer' but the religious community is apparently shamed, going away 'one by one, beginning with the elders'. They have been challenged by Jesus in public and, as a direct result, put to shame.

Taken together, these three stories suggest that Jesus was prepared both to affirm and to challenge religious communities. In them he affirmed communal practices when they did not conflict with the demands of communal compassion, but challenged them sharply when they did. The virtues identified at an individual level in the healing stories (compassion, care, faith and humility) are supplemented at a community level with sharp challenges, or even denunciations. For communities can act badly.

In the context of HIV, even church communities, sadly, can act badly. If they are to become genuinely compassionate, as Jesus still requires them to be, and indeed if they are to become effective agents in HIV prevention, they still need to be challenged sharply. Fidelity, truth-telling and, above all, compassion should properly be marks of the Church.

Part 5
SEXUALITY AND FAMILIES

Sex selection

1996

———•◆•———

What should we make of the news that a US clinic is making a new technique available to couples for them to choose the sex of their baby?

The technique aims to separate sperm prior to artificial insemination, allowing people the choice of a male or female. It is apparently most successful for choosing girls (92 per cent success rate), but also considerably better than chance for boys (72 per cent success rate). The clinic offering this technique has so far helped nearly 200 couples to make this choice upon purely social grounds.

Of course, there are sometimes good medical grounds for wishing to choose the sex of a baby. For couples with a family history of a serious sex-linked genetic disease this new technique could be very important. Instead of risking having a baby with the disease or alternatively of having an abortion following prenatal screening, they will now be able to use this technique for improving their chances of avoiding the disease.

However, such genetic diseases are (fortunately) relatively uncommon. Instead, the main demand for this technique is likely to come from couples with purely social grounds for sex selection. Perhaps they already have four boys and desperately want to have a girl, or four girls but desperately want a boy. Perhaps, like a recent couple, they had such a girl, but she died. Or perhaps they are a couple (or even a single person) who just don't fancy a boy . . .

The further this list is extended the more worried many of us become. Is it really for us to choose the sex of a baby in this way? The gift of having a baby is fast being replaced with 'new techniques for reproduction'. We are progressively treating human life as a commodity, just as we have made nature around us into a commodity. The Brave New World that Aldous Huxley terrifyingly predicted half a century ago is now becoming a reality.

Before jumping to this conclusion an important distinction needs to be made between what is forbidden in law and what we forbid ourselves as Christians. Abortion is a good example. Like many other Anglicans (but, of course, not all) I supported the legalization of abortion in Britain in 1968. Even though I am unhappy with the current levels of abortion and believe that some resort to it too readily, I still have no desire whatsoever to return to a country with women dying from illegal abortions. Nonetheless, my wife and I never contemplated resorting to an abortion ourselves.

This distinction is important because strong, publicly acceptable reasons have to be advanced for forbidding something in law within a democracy. And it is not sufficient in a pluralist society simply to say that something should be forbidden because it runs contrary to Christian belief. It is surprising how often Christians miss this point. Perhaps our blasphemy laws protecting specifically Christian beliefs (a relic from a less pluralist society) have misled us here.[1]

As the law stands it appears that this new technique is not illegal. For example, the HFEA has no power to forbid it since it does not involve IVF or (for an existing couple) donated sperm. The HFEA would need new powers to forbid it in law and it would need good reasons for being given such powers. But are there such good reasons?

It could be argued that, if this technique were widely used, it would create serious imbalances in the population. So the common good requires us to forgo such choices made upon purely social grounds. This argument might apply in urban China with its one-child policy or in those parts of the world where boys are valued more highly than girls. Yet it is hard to see that it applies to modern Britain. Presumably only a small number of couples would actually use the technique and there is little reason to believe that their choices would be skewed in favour of one gender. It can scarcely be made illegal in Britain on this ground.

Again, it could be argued that the technique is still unsafe. Lord Winston has indeed raised doubts about its safety. Interestingly (as a practising Orthodox Jew) he sees this as the *only* relevant ethical objection to the technique. Other medical scientists disagree with him about the risk involved here. I am not remotely qualified to comment. However, since some 200 babies have already been born using this technique, presumably it will soon become evident whether this risk is real or not. For the moment, unless there is real evidence of risk, it is difficult to see that it should actually be made illegal.

Another reason has already been mentioned – this technique treats babies as commodities. Perhaps it does, but it would be dangerous to have laws about this. Doubtless people have babies for all sorts of strange reasons, but most of us would hate to live in the sort of repressive country that forbade them from doing so. Laws in democratic countries should forbid, at most, only means that are both intrusive and unnecessary. Yet this technique is hardly very intrusive. Again, this is not a safe ground for making it illegal.

Even if this new technique remains legal, should Christians make use of it on anything other than medical grounds? A fundamental Christian belief is that a baby is a gracious gift from the God of love made known to us in Jesus Christ. As Christians we do disagree with each other about the status of embryos and whether or not to legalize abortion, but not about the status of babies. All babies – boys and girls, disabled and able – are children of God and should be treated equally. While this belief does not require us to reject this new technique as wholly unchristian, it might make us pause before endorsing too enthusiastically its use upon purely social grounds.

Yet I believe that there may still be some compassionate and pastoral reasons for using this technique beyond purely medical grounds – providing it is shown to be safe. The couple who tragically lost their daughter cannot, of course, replace her, but I do not regard their longing to have another girl as itself wrong. If they can be helped safely, why not?

Defending the family
1998

———•◦•———

In the preparation periods before Lambeth Conferences rumours of imminent break-up are common. Before the 1988 Conference the issue of women priests and women bishops was rumoured to be the issue which would shatter the Anglican Communion. In earlier Conferences it was such issues as polygamy in Africa or ecumenical unions in India. In 1998 sexuality and, more specifically, homosexuality and the ordination of active homosexuals are apparently *the* issues which will finally cause the Communion to implode. Sex, gender and ordination do seem to be powerful agents of Lambeth Conference rumours.

Personally, I doubt if differences over homosexuality really will prove to be so catastrophic. The Communion, with its long history of living tolerantly with differences, may be more resilient than is often imagined. Of course, sexuality is bound to be a topic of contention. Everyone is an expert in this area and there are many strong and incommensurable opinions. However, even if it takes an International Commission to establish this, bishops will finally affirm together what they can and will agree to disagree on what they cannot. This has always been the approach of classic Anglicanism. In a divided and contentious secular world, Anglican comprehensiveness at its best has been an important Christian witness.

Yet the danger of Anglican comprehensiveness is that attention can too easily be focused upon points of radical disagreement. The minority issues of polygamy in the past and homosexuality in the present can too easily dominate agendas. As a result, broad areas of agreement are treated summarily and side-lined. In the process, the importance of the family for Anglicans everywhere in the Communion can receive far too little attention. So, just when the family is under increasing threat in many parts of the world, Anglicans find themselves talking about almost anything but the family.

How can we defend the family in practical ways that make sense in our pluralistic societies? What are the essential features of families from an intelligent Christian perspective? How do we make sense of families when most of us are aware of divorce and unmarried cohabitation in our own families? Without turning the Anglican Communion into a sect composed only of biblical literalists, how do we take the simultaneous demands of the Bible, Christian faith and secular experience seriously?

These questions have been explored recently in the Family, Religion and Culture Project. Directed by the veteran pastoral theologian Professor Don Browning of the University of Chicago Divinity School, eight books have been published from this Project during the last two years. Taken together they give a remarkable overview of the social and theological debate about the family in the modern USA. They also offer thinking Christians everywhere serious ways of defending the family even as it continues to evolve in the modern world.

At the heart of the Family, Religion and Culture Project is a conviction that the family should be defended robustly by Christians, despite the fact that in the name of the Bible it has often been distorted in the past. In the foundation book for the series, *From Culture Wars to Common Ground: Religion and the American Family Debate*,[1] edited by Don S. Browning, the contributors summarize their main claim:

> The fundamental family issue of our time may be how to retain and honour the intact family without turning it into an object of idolatry and without retaining the inequalities of power, status, and privilege ensconced in its earlier forms.

The changes in US society affecting the family are obvious. One out of two marriages ends in divorce and almost one in three children is born outside marriage. Yet the USA is still a church-going country and over two-thirds of all marriages take place in churches and synagogues. Second and even third marriages regularly take place in Christian churches there. Those writing for the Project, largely drawn from liberal churches, are well aware of these facts when they seek to defend what they rather clumsily call the 'intact' family – by which they mean families in which children are brought up by both of their biological parents. Not wishing in any way to discriminate against other families (and divided among themselves on such issues as homosexuality), they still believe that it is vital for churches to encourage intact families, if necessary with help from the law.

They outline a series of practical aims and objectives:

1 Churches should defend, not patriarchal families, but more equal families which share and care for their own biological children. Poverty, delinquency, child abuse, poor health and a general lack of social function are strongly associated with families that are no longer intact. Churches should not be afraid to say that a massive social experiment in sexual permissiveness and individualism seems to have produced disastrous results, not least for children.

2 Churches should not copy Promise Keepers by turning uncritically to so-called 'biblical values'. For these liberal-minded Christians, as surely for most Anglicans, the patriarchy of many parts of the Bible belongs, like slavery, to the ancient world and not to the modern world. They are also well aware that the family has differed at many points in US history (often justified by different parts of the Bible) and will doubtless continue to change in the future.

3 Churches should develop positive theological defences of the family. The authors are particularly attracted to the biblical idea of covenant. Just as God voluntarily makes a two-way covenant with us, so we should have a corresponding covenant with each other and with our children. Christian marriage is not just a private agreement between two people, but a public covenant involving the whole community, with promises made by couples to each other and to any children they may bring into the world.

4 It is right to use civil society and even the law to protect and promote marriage. Partly this should be done through education in state schools. The authors challenge the idea that schools

should be 'neutral' on this issue. Partly it should be done through increasing tax incentives for those who are married and even by being prepared to make divorce more difficult to obtain.

5 Finally, churches themselves should be much more pro-active in creating a culture of what they term 'critical familism'. The authors argue that too many churches do not give adequate marriage preparation for engaged couples and do even less with youth and teenagers. Instead, churches could do much more to foster a family culture, at the same time offering a robust critique of negative images of the family which appear too often on television and in films.

Now, of course, all of this is very American. So can it be applied to Lambeth? I believe that it can. Some of the social features will doubtless differ from one country to the next – in Britain, for example, divorce is lower but illegitimacy higher – yet globalization means that few of us remain unaffected by change. In cities around the Anglican Communion there are increasing threats to Christian marriage and to those biological families which stay faithfully together. Evidence of teenage delinquency, single-parent poverty and child abuse can be found in many countries from Africa to Australia to South America. These are not just US ills. They are the ills of a global village. A clear and critical Christian voice, as well as practical action, is desperately needed throughout the Anglican Communion.

Can the Lambeth bishops manage to bring new and fresh vision to the family in the modern world? I genuinely hope that they can. If bishops can accept patiently their obvious differences on such issues as homosexuality, then perhaps their convictions about marriage and the family can be heard more clearly.[2] Most of the Lambeth bishops are themselves married. Unlike the Roman Catholic Church we do not have an episcopate with little personal experience of the frailties and challenges of married life. On the contrary, the Lambeth bishops abound with personal experience of faithful, committed and reciprocal marriage. Instead of dividing them, this could be an issue to unite them and to offer a confused world a note of real wisdom and practical guidance.

Rediscovering Christian faithfulness

2002

<hr/>

To the dismay of many Anglicans, homosexuality threatens to remain a major Anglican fault line. Is it possible that much of the current debate is missing an obvious point, namely that Christians do have something important to say about sexuality in general?

Allen Verhey in his new book *Remembering Jesus: Christian Community, Scripture, and the Moral Life*[1] argues that secular ethics is not simply to be dismissed or by-passed by Christians. At best, secular ethics can set minimum standards that everyone should accept. In sexual relationships (whether heterosexual or homosexual) this minimum standard is informed, uncoerced and competent consent. Yet this minimum standard, although essential, is not sufficient: for the continuing Christian tradition of 'good sex', faithfulness and not just consent is also crucial.

There is now enormous evidence that faithfulness between parents is crucial for the well-being of their children. Faithfulness may also be crucial for adults, whatever their sexual orientation. It is through faithfulness to another that we can discover love: both God's love for us and, in turn, a proper sense of self-love.

Allen Verhey is very committed to biblical theology and ethics, arguing that at the heart of responsible Christian ethics is a persistent attempt to 'remember Jesus' both through the Gospels and through the witness of the Early Church. Yet he is not convinced by those who attempt to derive 'moral rules' from the Bible, arguing that the Bible is often elusive on specific issues and in any case is not a rule book. So on gender and sexual issues he studiously avoids such rules, yet invites readers to remember Jesus' own faithful relationships with other people.

Faithfulness is a deeply theological and biblical notion. God is faithful to us and beckons us in turn to be faithful to God, to each other and to ourselves. In the Old Testament the Covenant is the symbol *par excellence* of God's faithfulness, and in the New Testament the symbol of God's faithfulness is the cross. In turn, a faithful Christian life is one that is faithful to God in Christ through the Spirit, that is faithful to other people, and that is faithful to self, especially by being faithful to God . . . In other words, the Christian life is properly seen as a circle of faithfulness. And intimate sexual relationships should always be included within this circle of faithfulness. Conversely, intimate sexual relationships deeply damage the Christian life if they are not so included.

The report *Human Sexuality* from the 1998 Lambeth Conference was concerned about 'Christ-like ways of living' and had one mention of faithfulness. Yet, ironically, faithfulness actually received more attention in the corresponding report at Lambeth 1988. The latter emphasized that 'the ingredients of Christian marriage are fidelity, trust, acceptance, an intention of permanence, mutual service and empowerment'. It also claimed that within the family (even within non-traditional families) individuals can 'understand the eternal ministry of Jesus as he feeds us with the bread of life, shelters us as children in his arms, teaches his faithful disciples and, having taken on human nature, ennobles all humanity'. It is difficult to find anything quite as theologically lyrical in Lambeth 98.

If the notion of faithfulness had less of a role in Lambeth 98 than in Lambeth 88, it has no role at all in the Lesbian and Gay Christian Movement's current Statement of Conviction. This simply states that members

> believe that human sexuality in all its richness is a gift of God gladly to be accepted, enjoyed and honoured, as a way of both expressing and growing in love, in accordance with the life and teaching of Jesus Christ; therefore it is their conviction that it is entirely compatible with the Christian faith not only to love another person of the same sex, but also to express that love fully in a personal, sexual relationship.

Although theologically lyrical, this statement is (at least in Allen Verhey's understanding) distinctly short of the minimum Christian standard of faithfulness. Doubtless the Lesbian and Gay Christian

Movement (LGCM) would respond that even though many of its members do live in faithful sexual relationships, such relationships are still condemned by sections of the Church.

It is worth comparing this with the position of the much-derided Anglican report *Something to Celebrate*.[2] This argued that many gay and lesbian partnerships do involve 'commitment and interdependence' and 'are able to create relationships of high quality, capable of expressing love, joy, peace, faithfulness, endurance, self-sacrifice and service to the outside world beyond their relationship'. It was precisely these virtues that *Something to Celebrate* saw as most characteristic of Christian marriage.

Perhaps if Anglicans took *Something to Celebrate* more seriously then real theological progress might be made. Supposing LGCM replaced the word 'personal' with 'faithful' in their statement and then challenged Lambeth 98 with its own logic. After all, Lambeth 98 stated as a matter of agreement between the bishops that:

> Clearly some expressions of sexuality are inherently contrary to the Christian way and are sinful. Such expressions of sexuality include promiscuity, prostitution, incest, pornography, paedophilia, predatory sexual behaviour, and sadomasochism (all of which may be heterosexual and homosexual) . . .

Now the logic of this point of agreement between traditionalist and non-traditionalist bishops alike is that there is a clear difference between homosexual (as well as heterosexual) behaviour that does involve such expressions and homosexual behaviour that does not. More than that, it is the first type of sexual behaviour that is identified as contrary to the Christian way and sinful. Just as clearly, on this logic, faithful sexual behaviour (heterosexual or homosexual) is not to be condemned in this way.

This point has usually been missed in the post-Lambeth 98 debate. Yet if taken seriously, it challenges Anglicans to treat homo-sexuals and heterosexuals equally and requires the same minimum Christian standards of both. Perhaps it really is time to ask both LGCM and Anglican 'traditionalists' to take the logic of Christian faithfulness more seriously in future debates.

Homosexuality and
the Anglican Family
2008

————•◆•————

The build-up to the Lambeth Conference 2008 is repeating patterns established immediately before the two previous Conferences. Leading up to 1988 it was feared that the ordination of women as priests would split the Anglican Communion. Robert Runcie had to use his remarkable diplomatic skills attempting to avert this. Ten years later it was women as bishops (before the Conference) and homosexuality (during it), with George Carey deploying his considerable strategic skills. Now we are hoping that Rowan Williams's well-honed theological skills will save the Anglican Communion in the aftermath of Gene Robinson's ordination as bishop.

Yet the reality is that Anglicanism has not been a Communion for years. Following the ordination of women as priests, a sizeable minority of clergy within almost every diocese in the Church of England no longer communicates with the majority that accepts women as priests – a pattern now replicated elsewhere in the world. The two groups communicate and affirm their ordination vows at separate services on Maundy Thursday and are served by different bishops. Now, following the ordination of Gene Robinson, the openly gay Bishop of New Hampshire, the Primates no longer receive Communion together. The Anglican 'Communion' clearly no longer exists in any meaningful sense. Strongly held views on the issue of homosexuality simply cannot be reconciled.

Two recent books by opposing groups of Anglican theologians demonstrate this clearly. *God, Gays and the Church: Human Sexuality and Experience in Christian Thinking*,[1] edited by Lisa Nolland, Chris Sugden and Sarah Finch, strongly expresses one side of the divide. In preparation for the 1998 Lambeth Conference

Chris Sugden and Vinay Samuel co-edited *Anglican Life and Witness*.[2] It offered a range of evangelical scholarship, with both a traditionalist declaration on human sexuality ('The St Andrew's Day Statement') and some powerful dissenting positions, not least that of Professor Oliver O'Donovan. It was widely read by the bishops and both editors were themselves highly influential, especially among traditionalists at the Conference.

Ahead of the 2008 Lambeth Conference Dr Sugden (now Executive Secretary of Anglican Mainstream and actively organizing the July meeting of traditionalist bishops in Jerusalem), together with Dr Lisa Nolland (a consultant for Anglican Mainstream) and the publisher Sarah Finch, has edited a decidedly more polemical book. Shocked by the February 2007 General Synod debate about human sexuality, the editors seek directly to challenge 'the activist gay lobby' that they believe dominated this debate and 'to redress the balance . . . [of] one-sided testimony'.

The first section of *God, Gays and the Church*, entitled 'Narratives', focuses upon post-gay and post-lesbian testimonies, given at a fringe meeting organized by Anglican Mainstream before the General Synod debate. They tend to be anecdotal and quite strongly worded. For example, the Texan Michael Goeke writes: 'Let me just say "THANK YOU" to my wife, and my parents and family, and my friends, who cared enough about me to offend me . . . when I left my wife to pursue homosexuality.'

Perhaps these testimonies were given by people who were simply mistaken about their same-sex attraction and had come to realize that they were not gay or lesbian after all. To address this possibility, the second section on 'Genetics' consists of an article by a New Zealand scientist, Neil Whitehead, arguing that same-sex attraction 'is neither innate nor immutable, and the degree of hidden change in the population [away from it] is generally considerably underestimated'. In the third section a Californian psychologist, Joseph Nicolosi, sets out his theory of 'Reparative therapy of male homosexuality'.

Considered on their own these three sections still raise a problem. There may be many people troubled about their sexual identity, some of whom will eventually want to question the validity of their same-sex attraction. Reparative therapy (or something like

it) may well help them. Similarly, many young people live for
several years as committed vegetarians or even vegans before
rejoining the dominant meat-eating culture. People change and
can be helped when they decide that they *want* to change. Yet
something more is needed to show why gays and lesbians *ought*
to change.

The 'something more' is provided in the fourth section on
'Biblical theology'. Robert Gagnon, Professor of New Testament
at Pittsburgh Theological Seminary, offers an extended 'rebuttal'
of a paper on gay liberation given to the Anglican Church of
Canada, arguing that 'a prohibition of "committed" homosexual
unions is both reasonable and scriptural'. A crucial point emerges
from the rebuttal, namely: *if* Scripture is understood in this
particular way then homosexual practice is an abomination
and *this* is why gay and lesbian people *should* want to change . . .
however painful the process of change might be. This widely
contended conviction is pivotal to the whole book.

In contrast there is *The Bible, the Church and Homosexuality*,[3]
edited by Nicholas Coulton, Sub-Dean of Christ Church, Oxford.
He has gathered together liberal-minded colleagues associated
with Oxford in a book that is less strident than *God, Gays and the
Church* but just as determined.

Christopher Rowland, Dean Ireland Professor of the Exegesis
of Holy Scripture, argues that, contrary to the cliché, Christianity
is not a religion of the book:

> Christianity did not start like that, and to seek to be true to the
> method of Paul as he interprets Scripture is to recognize that what
> is central in the life of Christians is obedience to the divine Spirit
> in our time.

He is unimpressed when Christians simply take two verses from
Romans and 1 Corinthians as 'law code' about homosexuality.

Marilyn McCord Adams, Regius Professor of Divinity, and Jane
Shaw, Dean of New College, both offer accounts of how acceptable
patterns of sexuality changed over time, both within the Bible
and within subsequent church history. Neither dwells long on
homosexuality, but their message is clear: reifying particular forms
of 'family' is not faithful to biblical or post-biblical tradition. Jane

Shaw is particularly critical of the House of Bishops' original 1991 *Issues in Human Sexuality* and its successor in 2003, arguing that it sought to reinstate the 'presumption that the clergy should be held to a different standard of moral behaviour from that required of lay people . . . shattered at the Reformation . . . [and] dispelled in the modern Church'.

Margaret Bedggood, recently retired Professor of Law at Waikato, human rights expert and activist and Third-Order Franciscan, argues with passion that the Church should embrace human rights more actively. And she is deeply embarrassed that so many theologians are scathing of the whole notion of human rights and that bishops have sought to exempt the Church from human rights in its employment policies enshrining sexual and gender discrimination.

Ironically, both books start with a foreword by a serving diocesan bishop supporting what follows. The Bishop of Winchester commends *God, Gays and the Church*, writing that 'some of the essays that follow offer experience of the transforming power of the Gospel', whereas the Bishop of Oxford commends *The Bible, the Church and Homosexuality*: 'They combine a deep understanding of the past with a passion to communicate the message of Christ faithfully today.'

In more colonial times it might have been possible for an Archbishop of Canterbury to quell such profound differences, for example when the Bishop of Hong Kong ordained a woman in the 1940s. However, in a post-colonial age this is no longer an option, even with the combined skills of recent archbishops. Why should the Americans conform when they have been instrumental in effecting what they believe are essential changes – democratically elected bishops, women as priests and bishops, and the democratically elected Gene Robinson? Why should Nigerians conform when everything in their theology and culture tells them that homosexuality (probably orientation as well as practice) is deeply sinful and an abomination?

Anglicans may simply have grown up. In a post-colonial age it seems unlikely that we can ever be a Communion again when there are so many areas of potential conflict – ordination, doctrine, sexuality, liturgy, authority, politics – any of which could fracture the Communion further. Of course, 'we' (the true Anglicans) could exclude everyone with whom we disagree, but that is simply a recipe for constant schism, as Pentecostals around the world have experienced.

Perhaps we need to use a different biblical model . . . family rather than communion. If the Anglican Communion is now permanently fractured, we might think of ourselves instead as the Anglican Family.

The model or metaphor of 'family' can be used rather sloppily in churches. Much to the annoyance of some parishioners, 'family' worship or 'family' communion can become little more than a cliché. The church as a 'family' can also be an excuse for petty and ill-mannered behaviour. In reality we all know that families are highly complex in pluralist societies and can be deeply problematic.

Family resemblance theory offers a more robust model. It suggests that particular families may have shared characteristics that identify them as families even when there is no single characteristic held by every member of that family. So some families have outstanding musical, artistic, social and intellectual skills. Yet there may be no member of the family that has all of these skills and no single skill that every family member has.

This theory helps to resolve the dilemma of Archbishop Michael Ramsey and, later, Professor Stephen Sykes. Michael Ramsey tried, but ultimately failed, to find a distinctive Anglican theology shared by all Anglican theologians. In his early work[4] Stephen Sykes tried to find a distinctive Anglican pattern of doctrine derived from a (then) widely shared use of the Book of Common Prayer. In more pluralist times it seems that Anglicans may have shared characteristics but that there are few, if any, characteristics that every Anglican shares. We draw variously and differently from a common heritage.

For the last 15 years I have been lecturing at Canterbury and elsewhere around the Anglican Family – including Moore College in Sydney, United Theological College (UTC) in Bangalore, Newton College in Papua New Guinea and Church Divinity School of the Pacific (CDSP) in Berkeley. In each I have encountered an abundance of differing and sometimes conflicting characteristics (only one of these colleges accepts the ordination of gays and only two the ordination of women), while still seeing all as parts of the same Anglican Family. At each I have seen at least one abiding Anglican emphasis: at Moore upon marriage and family life; at UTC upon the socially disadvantaged (especially the Dalits); at Newton upon a developing theological education in a country where tertiary education is still a privilege; and at CDSP upon inclusiveness and the changing role of women.

There are occasions when families do not talk to each other and have deep tensions and rivalries. Within families sexuality frequently engenders deep tensions, in the past on issues such as divorce or cohabitation, but in the present on single parenthood or homosexuality. Yet they remain families whether they want to be or not. Family members can make pompous statements such as 'I am no longer your sister.' Yet they obviously are. Likewise in the Anglican Family exclusion makes little sense and the Lambeth Conference can survive as a less formal family gathering whether or not the bishops share communion or agree about anything much.

The Anglican Family worldwide can be seen to flourish in many different ways, even within parts of its extended family, such as the Methodist Church, that have developed a separate ecclesial identity. In turn, the Anglican Family can also be seen to be a part of the extended Catholic Family, whatever recent popes have thought about the validity of Anglican orders or shared communion.

All Anglicans have a common genetic link with the Church of England but they have expressed their inheritance differently and, however much we may regret this, we are now unlikely ever again to be a Communion. Yet perhaps that can free us to be something else. If we are a Family, not a Communion, we need not strive for conformity. Why should families agree about everything? We can be free to explore shared convictions with like-minded family members around the world without denigrating other family members who do not share these convictions. The Evangelical Fellowship of the Anglican Church has wisely done this for years. Now others might do the same. As a genuinely post-colonial Church the Anglican Family would learn to move beyond power and authority . . . no more Lambeth Resolutions or Windsor Process.

Instead we might discover the joys of sharing and learning from different members of the same family . . . coming together when we want but not when we don't.

We might even rekindle some of the genuine family friendship and affection that I have seen so often in my own travels.

Part 6

ASSISTED DYING

Physician-assisted suicide

1996

———◆—————

Tucked away in the 'News in Brief' section of newspapers in August was a small item about the controversial American Dr Jack Kevorkian. Sometimes dubbed 'Dr Death', he has personally organized 35 physician-assisted suicides. Despite the fact that these are still illegal in the United States, he has yet to be successfully prosecuted. Juries simply refuse to find him guilty.

As in Britain, so in the USA there is widespread public support for euthanasia. A recent Gallup poll here suggested that three-quarters of the population supported physician-assisted suicide. A clear majority in all age groups approved, but among those aged 18–29 years support reached almost four-fifths.[1] Since a majority of the population here still claims church membership, Dr Kevorkian's activities may well be supported by many active Christians. Certainly a number of Dutch church groups have given support to the widespread toleration of active euthanasia in their country.

In June an editorial in the *British Medical Journal* (*BMJ*) depicted Dr Kevorkian as 'a medical hero'. To the dismay of a number of palliative care specialists who have since written letters to the editor, this highly influential journal has for some time been championing the cause of physician-assisted suicide. Following the acquittal back in 1992 of Dr Cox, who gave a terminally ill woman (on her request) life-shortening but non-palliative medication, the *BMJ* editor instructively argued that: 'More perhaps than any other, Britain is a post-religious society, where theological notions like the sanctity of life should not be overvalued . . . More and more doctors do seem to consider euthanasia acceptable in strictly defined circumstances.' And the editorial of *The Lancet* argued at the time that the BMA should 'look again across the North Sea [i.e. to Holland] and abandon the unsympathetic public line to which we have been exposed in the past few days'.

The Institute of Medical Ethics (IME), whose director, Kenneth Boyd, is himself an ordained Church of Scotland minister, has also expressed sympathetic views. A majority of the IME's 1990 working party held that:

> the doctor, acting in good conscience, is ethically justified in assisting death if the need to relieve intense and unceasing pain or distress caused by an incurable illness greatly outweighs the benefit to the patient of further prolonging his life.

They insisted, however, that it is important that the 'sustained wishes' of the patient on this issue should be known to the doctor. A key difference between physician-assisted suicide and other forms of direct euthanasia, such as shortening the life of the terminally comatose, is that the active co-operation of patients is clearly required.

Should British Anglicans also support physician-assisted suicides? Among theologians and senior clergy only few believe that they should. The Swiss Catholic theologian Hans Küng has reached this conclusion, as has Anglican theologian Paul Badham at Lampeter. In the past, Dean Inge at St Paul's Cathedral and Bishop Alastair Haggart in Scotland also did. Professor Badham has argued in print that we might even devise a liturgical setting for physician-assisted suicide, with a Eucharist immediately preceding it.[2] For him the proper response of Christian love is not to allow medical science tirelessly to postpone death. For the Christian, death eventually is to be welcomed. In the context of a terminal illness, the precise moment of death can rightly be chosen to help both patients and their families to accept death and the new life that it brings.

However, the latest news item about Dr Kevorkian might give us pause. His most recent patient, Judith Curren, 42, an overweight nurse from Pembroke, Massachusetts, may simply have been depressed about her obesity and not suffering from any terminal illness. Apparently the coroner could find no evidence of disease. A similar case occurred in the Netherlands last year. A doctor helped a chronically depressed middle-aged woman to end her life without any evidence that she was terminally ill. It remains to be seen whether Dr Kevorkian will be prosecuted.[3] The Dutch doctor was, but again the jury refused to convict him.

What is particularly confusing for Christian ethics about Dr Kevorkian is his moral character. He has shown that he is repeatedly prepared to risk imprisonment for his actions and yet apparently he makes no financial gain from them. He displays an extraordinarily high level of moral courage and conviction with an ascetic altruism and, unlike most of the rest of us, is prepared actively to challenge the law to ease the suffering of others.

Nevertheless, I worry that Anglicans might repeat the mistakes of the 1960s resulting from the Abortion Act. Then, as now, there was considerable media pressure for a change in law based upon difficult cases. It was argued then that abortion to relieve suffering had popular support and that the law at the time placed doctors in an impossible position. Yet, as I argued three weeks ago,[4] a liberty was soon turned into a licence. The Abortion Act allowed for serious grounds for abortion but was soon widely interpreted as allowing abortion on almost any grounds, especially in the first trimester.

Could we ever be confident that a law allowing physician-assisted suicide, let alone more direct forms of euthanasia, would not follow a similar path? A liberty allowed on deeply compassionate grounds might again become a licence allowed on almost any grounds. The powerless, the depressed, the disabled and the vulnerable might soon become suitable cases for euthanasia. It is instructive that the latest Kevorkian case has received so little attention. In contrast, cases which seem to support euthanasia have received enormous publicity.

It is precisely this question that has delayed legislators in many parts of the world. Legislation in the Northern Territory in Australia and in Oregon in the USA has been met by considerable anxiety from other states. Everyone watches the Dutch, but even they have so far acted only on a negative basis. In effect they have an agreement not to prosecute if proper procedures are observed by doctors involved in euthanasia.[5] Even then, the experience of the Dutch continues to cause anxiety. A small percentage of their recorded cases of euthanasia do not conform to their own procedures, and yet the doctors involved are seldom prosecuted. And the Royal Dutch Medical Association has now set up a review with the intention of considerably reducing these procedures, so that individual doctors conforming to guidelines would no longer have to get the prior agreement of the prosecuting authorities.

If we believe that life is finally God-given and that we should be particularly concerned about the plight of the marginalized and vulnerable, then I believe that we should proceed with real caution in this area. We may well agree with Baroness Warnock that a mandatory life-sentence is unjust for those involved in physician-assisted suicides. We may also agree that it is wrong to prolong the life of those in a permanent vegetative state. Yet we should, I believe, be cautious about supporting a change in the law on compassionate grounds only to repeat the mistakes we made over the Abortion Act.

The compassionate case for assisted suicide

2001

———————◆·◆·◆———————

Voluntary euthanasia is back in the news. The VES is sponsoring a challenge to the law through Diane Pretty, a sufferer from advanced motor neurone disease.

Last year the BMA held a special conference on physician-assisted suicide. Following changes in the law in Oregon and the Netherlands, there was a strong feeling among some doctors and patient groups that doctors, or even relatives, should be allowed to assist the terminally ill to choose their own moment of death. Modern medicine, they argued, is in danger of needlessly prolonging the lives of those terminally ill patients who wish to end their lives but cannot do so for themselves.

One of the most moving moments of the conference was a scene enacted by two professional actors, one playing the role of a doctor and the other a patient with motor neurone disease who wanted to be helped to die. This disease is particularly tragic because the sufferer usually remains alert mentally (as Professor Stephen Hawking has shown) while slowly and inexorably deteriorating at a physical level. The end stage of the disease can be quite horrible, with the sufferer choking or suffocating.

The doctors at the conference finally decided not to support physician-assisted suicide as part of BMA policy. They feared the effect that this might have on other doctor–patient relationships and its wider implications for society at large. Yet they did affirm that medical treatment and even artificial feeding can properly be withdrawn from patients when these lack any real benefit for them. And they were well aware that their decision on physician-assisted suicide was only a rejection 'for the moment'.

Anyone who has experienced the death of a family member at the end of a protracted terminal illness is likely to know the dilemma at first hand. Relatives and even the patient him- or herself may openly say that they wish that the process of dying could be hastened. Despite all the real achievements of the hospice movement and palliative medicine, a slow, protracted death can still seem so cruel and pointless.

Many Christians will be sympathetic with Brian Pretty's plea that he should be allowed to help Diane to die with dignity when they both believe that the time is right. He does not wish to break the law and risk imprisonment (although, in reality, courts have recently been lenient with other relatives). Instead, he and Diane are challenging the law in terms of the new Human Rights Act.

It must be for lawyers to speculate about whether or not they are likely to succeed in this challenge.[1] The Human Rights Act certainly does not specify that people have a right to choose the moment of their death. Yet it does say that they have a right to life and, more relevantly, a right not to have degrading treatment. I suspect that the judiciary will be sympathetic (as they were earlier in the case of Anthony Bland)[2] and will try to find a way of allowing her to die and perhaps even of overlooking complicity on his part. Time will show. However, from a perspective of Christian ethics, would this be right?

So far most of us working in Christian ethics have resisted supporting voluntary euthanasia or assisted suicide. Some take a strongly principled stance that the taking of innocent human life in any form is wrong (even when the person concerned agrees). Others of us are more concerned about consequences. If assisted suicide is allowed in such cases, then what else will follow? In the Netherlands a long-term acceptance of voluntary euthanasia has also resulted in widespread involuntary euthanasia, in a failure to develop adequate palliative care and (arguably) in some old people living in fear of being pressurized into euthanasia.

All of this has convinced me to be very cautious in this area. Yet at the same time Christians should not simply ignore the plea of people like Diane and Brian Pretty (whatever pressure group is behind them). The Gospel for the coming Sunday could not be more apposite. St Luke tells the story of a woman who came to Jesus for deliverance from a long-standing affliction. Jesus responded at once, despite it being the Sabbath, on compassionate grounds, ignoring the scruples of the principled religious authorities of the times. He set her free from her bondage, 'all his opponents were put to shame' and 'the entire crowd was rejoicing at all the wonderful things that he was doing' (Luke 13.17).

Now, of course, the 'deliverance' for Diane Pretty will be an early death rather than a cure. This is an important difference but not a conclusive one. The ineluctable nature of motor neurone disease does have a special horror for many sufferers, so the prospect of being spared from its final stages may represent a very real deliverance for them. If they can be helped, without harming others, then Christian compassion seems to demand that they should be.

More strongly than that, religious authorities who stand in their way risk Jesus' stark denunciation. To put it bluntly, religious people should not require other people to suffer just to satisfy their own principles. Doubtless the leader of the synagogue [as noted earlier] was trying to uphold a deeply held principle defending the Sabbath. Yet Jesus in this story saw the claims of compassion as being far more important. Likewise, there are real fears of slipping principles in defending 'deliverance' for Diane Pretty. However, the demands of compassion are also crucial.

We do need the protection of law here. If nobody is to be prosecuted for assisting others to die, then the risks of abuse are only too obvious. Fine legal distinctions need to be made about whether Diane Pretty is to have treatment and artificial feeding withdrawn (as is her legal right already), to receive large amounts of sedatives or opiates which may shorten her life, or to be given access to drugs that would end her life (which may set a dangerous precedent). Similarly, legal distinctions need to be made for Brian Pretty. This is essential if other people are to be helped and protected. However, if this can be done safely (even on a case-by-case judicial basis as now happens with persistent vegetative state patients), then Christian compassion does seem to require it.

Compassion and euthanasia

2005

———————

Three years ago (and a year before her death from natural causes) I was asked by the VES to make a submission to the House of Lords on Diane Pretty's behalf. She was at the time making her application for a judicial review challenging the law banning euthanasia in this country.

I had argued a few months earlier in *Church Times* that Diane Pretty's predicament ought to be treated with compassion, especially by religious people, and that careful legal attempts to help her and her husband should be encouraged. I was also aware that it tends to be religious and secular lobby groups with strong opinions who make submissions to such reviews. As a result, compassionate views tend to get under-represented.

However, I did explain to VES that, like the Church of England's House of Bishops, I am not actually a supporter of changing the law in this area. Our opposition to legalizing voluntary euthanasia is itself based upon compassionate grounds. We fear the harm to the common good that may happen if the law were to be changed: allowing intentional killing in a clinical context could endanger the protection that the law gives, damage the doctor–patient relationship, and make other vulnerable people more vulnerable.

VES responded that they were happy for me to make my opposition to legalizing voluntary euthanasia clear in the submission. I also made the same point clear at the House of Lords Select Committee last week. What VES wanted me to show was simply that there are religious people who do support legalized voluntary euthanasia (just as there are secular people who do not). This should not become a battleground – what Americans term 'cultural wars' – between religious and secular people. After all, religious people were founding members of VES.

Compassion [as argued earlier] is a central virtue in many religious traditions. It may even be *the* most important. In the Gospels, especially, the ill and disabled came to Jesus begging for mercy and he responded. Today, compassion also deeply informs secular humanism in the West.

Given the tragic circumstances of people like Diane Pretty, it is difficult for compassionate people to disagree. She faced the horrifying possibility of choking to death having lost speech and mobility while remaining fully conscious to the end. Who wouldn't want to help her have a better death than this? Lord Joffe makes this point repeatedly to doctors coming before the current Select Committee.[1] In my personal view (I cannot speak for the bishops here) the current judicial situation in which so-called mercy-killers are treated leniently is both compassionate and justified. Equally, I think it is compassionate and justified not to prosecute relatives of the terminally ill travelling to Switzerland for 'aiding and abetting' under the Suicide Act or doctors in this country who act in good faith.

The 1998 Lambeth Conference of Anglican Bishops also reacted compassionately. Although opposed to legalizing euthanasia, they agreed that to withhold or withdraw excessive medical treatment or intervention (even life support) may be appropriate where there is no reasonable prospect of recovery. They also agreed that, when the primary intent is to relieve suffering and not to bring about death, it is right to provide alleviation of intolerable pain and suffering even if the side effects hasten the dying process.

Clashes between the good for particular individuals and the common good are notoriously difficult to resolve in medical ethics. In sub-Saharan Africa, for example, compassion requires that individuals living with HIV should not be stigmatized or lectured about sexual morality. Yet the common good requires that we try to eliminate this terrible virus, if necessary by using the public health weapons of moralizing and shaming. Or again, in a context of recent fears about the safety of the measles, mumps and rubella (MMR) vaccine, some parents concluded that it was better not to give their child the vaccine, albeit knowing that, if enough other parents did the same, immunity in the general population would be endangered.

These are not easy issues to resolve. For the moment, I fear damaging the common good if voluntary euthanasia were to be legalized. At the same time I am grateful for the judicial compassion that is increasingly shown in this country. I believe that it is thoroughly consonant with Christian faith.

Legalizing euthanasia?

2009

———•◆•———

The June Colloquium in Trinity, Dublin, that inspired this paper met at a particularly interesting time.[1] It was widely expected that the House of Lords was on the point of decriminalizing the act of helping the terminally ill to go abroad for assisted dying. British newspapers were full of stories and articles about assisted dying, many of them sympathetic to a change in law. This made the Colloquium both lively and topical.

Yet, as it happens, the House of Lords did no such thing. By a majority of 194 to 141 peers decided in early July to reject what many experts believed was a very serious chance to change the law. This decision had a knock-on effect upon the Law Lords. They had already started to consider the appeal of Debbie Purdy (who has MS) for written clarity from the Director of Public Prosecutions (DPP) of the grounds on which he would or would not prosecute those helping people to go abroad for assisted dying. Had the Falconer amendment been accepted, their judgment on this appeal would have been unnecessary. Once it was rejected they needed to act swiftly, since their roles were very soon to be replaced by the new Supreme Court. At the end of July they made their final and historic judgment to uphold Debbie Purdy's appeal.

For the last two decades the House of Lords has been agonizing about the possibility of legalizing euthanasia or assisted dying. Two House of Lords Select Committees have considered this at length, the first in the early 1990s with Archbishop John Habgood and the second a decade later with Bishop Christopher Herbert as members. The report of the first Select Committee came out unanimously against 'intentional killing' by doctors, but failed to reach agreement on the very issue that had generated the committee, namely what to do with those who are permanently comatose and insensate (PVS patients). The report of the second Select Committee was informative but largely descriptive, members having remained thoroughly divided on the propriety of assisted dying.

The context noted at the Colloquium in June was the rather obscure Coroners and Justice Bill. Within this a very significant and ingenious attempt was made to amend the Suicide Act of 1961. The amendment had some very powerful sponsors, including the former Lord Chancellor, Lord Falconer, and Baroness Jay, a prime minister's daughter and uniquely a former member of both of the Select Committees.

The proposed amendment also had considerable legal logic. The Suicide Act decriminalized suicide at a time when English courts had already become very reluctant to imprison those who attempted but failed to commit suicide. The Act was widely seen as a compassionate move which also recognized the futility of this law in the early 1960s. However, it remained an offence for anyone to encourage or assist someone to commit suicide. Suicide itself was decriminalized but (contrary to popular interpretation) it did not become a right with a corresponding duty for others to assist, encourage or even passively witness a suicide.

Five decades later practice has clearly changed. The amendment's sponsors argued, understandably, that further decriminalization is now needed, this time for those helping the terminally ill to commit (assisted) suicide and not simply for those attempting to commit suicide. With 115 cases of assisted suicide involving relatives and friends going to clinics in Switzerland (where assisted suicide was never made illegal) and no prosecutions to date in English courts, parts of the Suicide Act now look outdated and futile. Opinion polls also suggest widespread public sympathy (by churchgoers too) for those assisting the terminally ill in this way.

Lord Falconer and his fellow sponsors argued that legal clarity is needed. His amendment sought to introduce a careful procedure for checking that the individual concerned really is terminally ill, has capacity and has agreed freely in writing, and that this is all properly and independently witnessed. If the amendment had been passed then those following this procedure would no longer have risked prosecution (however unlikely that might actually be).

However, Baroness Professor Ilora Finlay, a renowned expert in palliative medicine, together with the lawyer Lord Carlile, argued at length in the House and the press that it was right to show compassion to relatives who take the terminally ill to Switzerland, but that it was important that the DPP continues to review cases carefully in order to ensure that no abuse is involved. They also argued that Lord Joffe's successive attempts to change the law demonstrated that there was a considerable slippery slope evident. If taking the terminally ill to Swiss clinics were to be decriminalized, how long would it be before clinics arose in Britain? If assisting those with capacity were to be decriminalized, what about those with limited capacity or lacking capacity? And if assisting the terminally ill to end their lives were to be decriminalized, what about those who were not terminally ill but had intractable pain, or disability, or depression, or discomfort, or financial ruin, or perhaps just a persistent capacity to embarrass or annoy others? Difficult cases notoriously can make bad laws.

It was public arguments such as these that seem to have convinced the peers. It is also important to note that peers themselves are now much more diverse than they were in the past, with some peers appointed specifically to represent people with serious disabilities (several of whom were outspoken in their opposition to the amendment). I suspect that their majority decision makes any change in English law in the immediate future within this vexed area less likely.

Yet the effect of Debbie Purdy's successful appeal has been to force the DPP to be more explicit about the grounds on which he is or is not prepared to bring a prosecution. In relation to Baroness Finlay and Lord Carlile's first point, the DPP will continue to review all cases in principle to ensure that no abuse is involved. None will be outside the law. He has had, though, to give published [albeit still interim, at the time of writing] details of the grounds on which prosecutions are likely to be brought. A DPP always has discretion not to prosecute even if a crime has apparently been committed. After 115 cases using this discretion he had previously given published grounds for his decision only once (in relation to Daniel James). Now he has been more explicit, specifying what factors could determine a prosecution (including whether a person stands to benefit financially from assisting a suicide, whether that person is not motivated solely by compassion, whether an individual wanting to die is under 18 or not deemed competent enough to have a clear and settled wish, or whether an individual has been persuaded or pressurized into committing suicide). This gives Debbie Purdy (and others) enough information to assess whether her husband is likely to be prosecuted if he does finally take her to Switzerland for assisted dying.

However, in relation to their second point, it is probably too early to know whether the Purdy judgment might precipitate such a slippery slope. The DPP's consultation on the interim policy for prosecutors on assisted suicide concluded by December 2009. In its submission the British Medical Association stated emphatically that its 'policy is firmly opposed to assisted suicide and to doctors taking a role in any form of assisted dying'. It also made clear that it 'is not seeking any change in UK legislation on this issue', while at the same time conceding that it was not actually opposed to the DPP's interim policy. The Church of England's Mission and Public Affairs Council's submission also emphasized that it 'believes that every suicide is a tragedy and that a caring society ought to ensure that anyone considering suicide is able to have ready access to life-affirming and life-enhancing support, counselling and medical and nursing care'. This submission recognized that some people do choose suicide and request others to assist them to do so, but maintained that 'we wish to respond to such people with compassion and empathy but we believe that compassion is best expressed by making every effort to dissuade them from committing suicide, not by assisting them'. Crucially, however, this submission also conceded that

> we recognise that some people will believe that they may best express genuine compassion by assisting a loved one to commit suicide ... we do not agree that compassion is best expressed in this way but neither do we believe that prosecution is appropriate in all cases.

Do both of these concessions (which I personally welcome) make a slippery slope more likely? It is worth noting that, when a similar Law Lords judgment in 1992 allowed the withdrawal of life-sustaining treatment (including artificial nutrition and hydration) from PVS patients, it was predicted that this would soon result in the involuntary euthanasia of, say, people with dementia. Yet so far this slippery slope has not emerged.

All of this needs to be put into the wider setting that informed the Colloquium. It is now firmly established in British law, as well as good medical practice set by the General Medical Council and the British Medical Association (the first the regulatory body for doctors and the second their union), that someone with capacity has the right to refuse life-sustaining treatment and that it would be an offence for a doctor to give treatment against the clear wishes of a patient. In addition, doctors, whatever their personal or religious views, must now respect valid advance directives (living wills) about refusing such treatment. There is also, as just mentioned, the 1992 Law Lords judgment allowing the withdrawal of artificial nutrition and hydration from PVS patients. Does all of this amount to assisted dying or even to euthanasia? And what about the so-called double effect when, for example, a doctor gives treatment to a patient in order to relieve severe pain while realizing that it may also shorten his or her life?

Much depends here upon definitions. Many definitions of euthanasia include intention and focus upon the deliberate foreshortening of life by medical means. As I will explain in a moment, I am not altogether convinced by them. My own definition of euthanasia is broader:

> Medical action or omission which knowingly results in the death of a person.

On this definition most or even all of the types of treatment or non-treatment in the previous paragraph (which many of us already support) are forms of euthanasia, as can be seen from Table 1 overleaf.

The two ends of the spectrum here are Daniel James and Anthony Bland. Daniel James was a 23-year-old who tragically broke his neck playing rugby and was severely paralysed as a result. He attempted to commit suicide several times. Earlier this year

Assisted dying

Table 1 Euthanasia

Patient \ Doctor	Takes action	Acts indirectly	Stops acting
Willing (and has capacity to decide)	Daniel James	Double effect	Ms B
Was willing at one time	Debbie Purdy	?Living will	Living will
Lacks capacity to decide	Involuntary euthanasia	?Anthony Bland	Anthony Bland

and 18 months after his accident, his parents helped to take him to the Swiss clinic Dignitas where he was given drugs to end his life. Despite the fact that he was not terminally ill the DPP in England decided, on the return of the parents from Switzerland, that it would not serve the public interest to prosecute them under the Suicide Act. The DPP would also have known that on compassionate grounds a jury was extremely unlikely to convict them or a judge to imprison them in these tragic circumstances. This is a very clear instance of assisting someone deliberately to fore-shorten life by medical means.

Anthony Bland was also a young man severely damaged at a sporting event, although in this case he was a spectator, not a player. He was crushed by a surging crowd at the Hillsborough Football Disaster in 1989 and lay in a fetal position with apparently no sensation whatsoever (his cortex had effectively been destroyed) for the next three years. He was fed through an intensive nursing regime of nasogastric tubes and evacuated using enemas. His parents repeatedly asked for this regime to be stopped and for him to be allowed to die. After a lengthy legal process the 1992 Law Lords judgment allowed this to happen and he died 11 days later (probably from kidney failure due to lack of hydration). The five Law Lords clearly found this decision difficult, but it did allow a number of other similar PVS patients to have their artificial nutrition and hydration withdrawn over the next two decades (although each case still needs to be brought for judicial review). Many have argued that such withdrawing (or omission) is quite different from the Daniel James situation and does not constitute a deliberate foreshortening of life by medical means.

But is this really so? There are some obvious differences between the two young men. Daniel James was evidently very determined and convinced about assisted dying, whereas there is no evidence that Anthony Bland had ever considered it. In addition, Daniel James's parents tried to dissuade him from assisted dying, whereas Anthony Bland's parents were the ones seeking an end to his life-sustaining treatment. Yet are the two cases really so different in other respects? The Law Lords judgment relating to Anthony Bland (which I supported on compassionate grounds) stretched legal and ethical logic. It does seem to me to be clear that the Law Lords 'wanted' something, namely to find a way of bringing Anthony Bland's 'life' (if that is what it was) to an end in a manner that did not set a precedent for non-PVS patients. Several of the Law Lords mentioned their uneasiness about straying into ethics and each used a rather different legal path to reach the same conclusion (namely, to agree with the family who wanted his life to end). Some lawyers have argued that this did indeed seem to be an attempt to justify an outcome legally that had been determined as 'right' in advance. So to depict this simply as a case of withdrawing futile treatment (which included artificial nutrition and hydration) appears to be less than the whole story. The Law Lords knew perfectly well that withdrawing such treatment would (and did) result in his death. The contention here is that they did not just 'know' this, they also 'wanted' it. Or to express this in terms of my definition of euthanasia, this was an omission which (very) knowingly resulted in the death of a person.

Ms B was again someone who was severely paralysed, although in this instance as the result of a stroke. Unlike Anthony Bland she was fully conscious and depended upon a ventilator to keep her alive. Eventually she asked to be taken off the ventilator and to be allowed to die. Again this led to a lengthy judicial process. Finally a very senior judge went to see her in hospital in order to determine whether she had capacity to understand fully the implications of this request. The judge decided that she did indeed and that the doctors and nurses must comply with her clear and persistent request whatever their personal beliefs (or hand her over to others who would comply with it – which is exactly what happened). As a result of this decision she was removed from the ventilator and died. Once again this was an omission which knowingly resulted in the death of a person, although, unlike Anthony Bland, the request had come from the patient herself and there is no evidence at all that the judge here 'wanted' her to die. However, the important point to note is that English law in this area is now unequivocal. Given such a clear and persistent request for withdrawal from a patient with full capacity, doctors and nurses cannot continue even with life-sustaining treatment. This form of euthanasia (if that is what it is) is mandatory.

If my definition of euthanasia and my interpretations of these cases are accepted, then it follows that standard modern medical practice in Britain already permits euthanasia. The question becomes not 'Should we legalize euthanasia?' but rather 'Where should we draw the line?' A variety of different answers will be given to this second question. That is as it should be. Christians are not united on this vexed issue. Nor is the general public. In reality every ethically responsible person (whether religious or not) needs to draw the line somewhere, since none would defend, say, Dr Harold Shipman's drastic foreshortening of hundreds of elderly (and some not so elderly) lives seemingly for his own satisfaction rather than for any benefit expressed by his patients. And even when religious leaders are broadly united (typically on the more conservative side of the debate) their parishioners are not. Paul Badham's position [noted on page 122] is often criticized by theologians, yet it does appear to be widely shared within many congregations (both Catholic and Protestant). Interestingly, Debbie Purdy herself, in the aftermath of her successful appeal, made it clear that she too wants a line to be drawn and is not in favour of anyone for any reason being allowed to take people to Switzerland for assisted dying without fear of prosecution. Instead, what she wants (and has now received) is a clearer line in writing drawn up by the DPP.

Having read the Purdy judgment carefully I have been impressed by the compassion, sensitivity and persuasiveness of the Law Lords. In my view peers in the House of Lords, including the Law Lords, have shown that they can balance the different demands of justice and compassion with considerable sensitivity. Like Baroness Finlay and Lord Carlile, I do wish cases still to be reviewed (compassionately) by the DPP and fear the consequences for other vulnerable people of changing the law.

If I understand the situation properly there is a very similar balance now in Ireland as well. In both countries, among doctors and lawyers especially, there is a reluctance actually to change the law or to use existing law to prosecute those who act compassionately. This may not be very tidy but it does balance competing (and perhaps incommensurable) demands from people at their most vulnerable.

Notes

Churchgoing and moral attitudes

1 Dartmouth: Social and Community Planning Research, 1996.
2 The results of this research project can be found in Robin Gill, *Churchgoing and Christian Ethics*, Cambridge: Cambridge University Press, 1999.
3 See Grace Davie, *Religion in Britain since 1945: Believing Without Belonging*, Oxford: Blackwell, 1994. For a more recent discussion, see Grace Davie, *The Sociology of Religion*, London: Sage Publications, 2007.

Is Christian ethics distinctive?

1 Edinburgh: Canongate Books, 1999.
2 *The Scotsman*, 23 August 1999, p. 13.
3 See Robin Gill, *Churchgoing and Christian Ethics*, Cambridge: Cambridge University Press, 1999, Chapter 1, for a critical review of Hauerwas's books.

Changing attitudes

1 For this and other church census data, see Robin Gill, *The 'Empty' Church Revisited*, Aldershot: Aldersgate, 2003.
2 Church of England Working Party on Family Life, *Something to Celebrate*, London: Church House Publishing, 1995.

Public theology

1 See Keith Ward, *God, Chance and Necessity*, Oxford: Oneworld Publications, 1996.
2 For example, see Duncan B. Forrester, *Christian Justice and Public Policy*, Cambridge: Cambridge University Press, 1997, and *Truthful Action: Explorations in Practical Theology*, Edinburgh: T. & T. Clark, 2000.
3 See further, James Mackey, *Power and Christian Ethics*, Cambridge: Cambridge University Press, 1994.

Gospel values and healthcare today

1 Wesley Carr, *Handbook of Pastoral Studies*, London: SPCK, 1997, p. 235.

2 A version of this paper was also included in Martyn Percy and Stephen Lowe (eds), *The Character of Wisdom: Essays in Honour of Wesley Carr*, Aldershot: Aldersgate, 2004.

3 I develop this approach further in Robin Gill, *Health Care and Christian Ethics*, Cambridge: Cambridge University Press, 2006.

4 Howard Clark Kee, *Medicine, Miracle and Magic in New Testament Times*, Cambridge: Cambridge University Press, 1986; Gerd Theissen, *The Miracle Stories of the Early Christian Tradition*, Edinburgh: T. & T. Clark and Philadelphia: Fortress Press, 1983.

5 John Pilch, *Healing in the New Testament: Insights from Medical and Mediterranean Anthropology*, Minneapolis: Fortress Press, 2000.

6 For a fine theological analysis of compassion, see Oliver Davies, *A Theology of Compassion*, London: SCM Press, 2001.

7 Tom L. Beauchamp and James F. Childress, *Principles of Biomedical Ethics*, Oxford and New York: Oxford University Press, 1994.

8 See Byron R. Johnson's very comprehensive review, *Objective Hope: Assessing the Effectiveness of Faith-based Organizations: A Review of the Literature*, Philadelphia: Center for Research on Religion and Urban Civil Society, University of Pennsylvania, 2001.

9 See Robin Gill, *Churchgoing and Christian Ethics*, Cambridge: Cambridge University Press, 1999, Chapters 5 and 6.

10 London: Constable, 1965.

11 Douglas A. Hicks, *Inequality and Christian Ethics*, Cambridge: Cambridge University Press, 2000.

The Human Rights Act

1 *The Times*, 2 October 2001.

2 I.e. 'The compassionate case for assisted suicide', in Part 6 of this book.

3 Cambridge: Cambridge University Press, 1992.

4 Margaret Bedggood provides a striking critique of churches along similar lines in Nicholas Coulton (ed.), *The Bible, the Church and Homosexuality*, London: Darton, Longman & Todd, 2005, pp. 80–99.

The Mental Capacity Bill

1 The Mental Capacity Act became law in 2007.

2 It has not changed to date.

3 The public debate here is ongoing, with the General Medical Council remaining very cautious.

The new genetics

1 The debate here is ongoing with, as yet, very few genetic conditions requiring disclosure from (still voluntary) DNA tests. However, the danger remains.
2 As happened the following year (see 'Drawing the line in fertility treatments' in Part 3).
3 In most countries, human reproductive cloning and gene modification remain illegal.
4 Paul Ramsey, *Fabricated Man*, New Haven: Yale University Press, 1970, p. 39.
5 Ramsey, *Fabricated Man*, p. 138.
6 Embryo selection using pre-implantation genetic diagnosis is now possible for some genetic conditions.

Allowing embryonic stem-cell research

1 This was a lecture given at the Royal Society, London, after the publication of the Donaldson Report.
2 Department of Health, *Stem Cell Research: Medical Progress with Responsibility* (The Donaldson Report), London: Department of Health, 2000; <http://www.dh.gov.uk/en/Publicationsandstatistics/Publications/PublicationsPolicyAndGuidance/DH_4065084>.
3 An important example is David Albert Jones, *The Soul of the Embryo: An Enquiry into the Status of the Human Embryo in the Christian Tradition*, London: Continuum, 2004.
4 Sometimes termed the 'gradualist' ethical approach.

Blocking embryonic stem-cell research

1 President Obama reversed this decision in 2009.
2 27 February 2002, <www.publications.parliament.uk/pa/ld/ldstem.htm>.

Human enhancement

1 <http://www.bma.org.uk/images/Boosting_brainpower_tcm41-147266.pdf>
2 Princeton, NJ: Princeton University Press, 2007.
3 The notion of the 'common good' is explored particularly well in David Hollenbach, *The Common Good and Christian Ethics*, Cambridge: Cambridge University Press, 2002.

Synthetic biology

1 London: Royal Academy of Engineering, 2009, <www.raeng.org.uk>.

Abortion dilemmas

1 Oxford: Oxford University Press, 1995.
2 London: Church Assembly Board of Social Responsibility, 1965.
3 She did continue to face the risk, but then had a spontaneous abortion of all the octuplets.

Drawing the line in fertility treatments

1 Today there is also pre-implantation genetic diagnosis.

Spare embryos

1 This has now been extended.
2 Rowan Williams, *Lost Icons*, Edinburgh: T. & T. Clark, 2000, pp. 46–7.
3 This was the position that the High Court judgment later reached (see 'Consent' in Part 4).

Human reproductive cloning

1 It was later discovered that the South Korean claims were fraudulent.
2 See 'Allowing embryonic stem-cell research' in Part 2.

Priorities in healthcare

1 For a full discussion, see John Butler, *The Ethics of Health Care Rationing: Principles and Practices*, London: Cassell, 1999.

Organ donation

1 The situation remains critical today.
2 The BMA and DoH remain at odds on this issue today.

Organ donation at Christmas

1 I.e. the previous piece, 'Organ donation'.

Seductive evil

1 Cambridge: Cambridge University Press, 2001.
2 Cambridge: Cambridge University Press, 2000.
3 See further, Christopher C. H. Cook, *Alcohol, Addiction and Christian Ethics*, Cambridge: Cambridge University Press, 2006.

Consent

1 The appeal was not successful (see further 'Spare embryos' in Part 3).
2 See further in 'Legalizing euthanasia?' in Part 6.
3 2003, <http://www.dh.gov.uk/en/Publicationsandstatistics/Publications/PublicationsPolicyAndGuidance/DH_4069253>.
4 See further James Mackey, *Power and Christian Ethics*, Cambridge: Cambridge University Press, 1994.

Impurity, sin and disease

1 London: Routledge and Kegan Paul, 1966.
2 She died in 2007 aged 86.

Trust in doctors

1 This remains the legal position.
2 Onora O'Neill, *Autonomy and Trust in Bioethics*, Cambridge: Cambridge University Press, 2002, and *A Question of Trust*, Reith Lectures, <www.bbc.co.uk/radio4/reith2002>.
3 2005, <www.publications.parliament.uk/pa/ld/ldasdy.htm>.
4 See further in 'Legalizing euthanasia?' in Part 6.
5 <www.dh.gov.uk/en/Consultations/closedconsultations/DH_4123863>.
6 The Act finally replaced this with 'the need for supportive parenting'.

Jesus, community compassion and HIV prevention

1 This piece was first given in 2007 at a theological consultation in South Africa organized by the Ecumenical Advocacy Alliance with help from UNAIDS, and then at an AIDS Day service in Canterbury Cathedral. An earlier version was published in Gillian Paterson (ed.), *HIV Prevention: A Global Conversation*, Geneva: EAA, 2009.
2 See, for example, Vincent Taylor, *The Gospel According to St Mark*, London: Macmillan, 1959, p. 186; W. D. Davies and Dale C. Allison Jr, *A Critical Commentary on the Gospel According to Saint Matthew*, Vol. II, Edinburgh: T. & T. Clark, 1991, pp. 10–11; Martin Noth, *Leviticus*, London: SCM Press, 1965, p. 106; and Gordon J. Wenham, *The Book of Leviticus*, London: Hodder & Stoughton, 1979, p. 195.
3 S. G. Browne, *Leprosy in the Bible*, London: Christian Medical Fellowship, 1970, p. 8.
4 James D. G. Dunn, 'Jesus and purity: an ongoing debate', *New Testament Studies*, vol. 48, 2002, p. 461.

5 See my 'AIDS, leprosy and the Synoptic Jesus', in Robin Gill (ed.), *Reflecting Theologically on AIDS: A Global Challenge*, London: SCM Press and Geneva: UNAIDS, 2007, p. 110.
6 See further Robin Gill, *Health Care and Christian Ethics*, Cambridge: Cambridge University Press, 2006.
7 Dunn, 'Jesus and purity', pp. 449–67.
8 See C. F. Evans, *Saint Luke*, London and Philadelphia: SCM Press and Trinity Press, 1990, p. 338.
9 C. K. Barrett, *The Gospel According to St John: An Introduction with Commentary and Notes on the Greek Text*, London: SPCK, 1967, pp. 490–3.

Sex selection

1 The common law offences of blasphemy and blasphemous libel were eventually abolished in England and Wales in 2008 following the introduction of the Racial and Religious Hatred Act in 2006.

Defending the family

1 Louisville, KY: Westminster John Knox Press, 1997.
2 In the event this did not happen, as can be seen from the next piece.

Rediscovering Christian faithfulness

1 Grand Rapids, MI: Eerdmans, 2002.
2 Church of England Working Party on Family Life, *Something to Celebrate*, London: Church House Publishing, 1995.

Homosexuality and the Anglican Family

1 London: The Latimer Trust, 2008.
2 London: SPCK, 1998.
3 London: Darton, Longman & Todd, 2005.
4 Stephen Sykes, *The Integrity of Anglicanism*, London and Oxford: Mowbray, 1978.

Physician-assisted suicide

1 See further Robin Gill, *Churchgoing and Christian Ethics*, Cambridge: Cambridge University Press, 1999, pp. 184f.
2 Most recently in Paul Badham, *Is there a Christian Case for Assisted Dying?* London: SPCK, 2009.

3 He was eventually sent to prison in 1999 for another case and was
not released until 2007.
4 I.e. 'Abortion dilemmas' in Part 3.
5 The situation changed in 2002 when a euthanasia law was introduced
in the Netherlands.

The compassionate case for assisted suicide
1 This legal challenge was not successful.
2 For Anthony Bland, see 'Legalizing euthanasia?' later in this section.

Compassion and euthanasia
1 Leading to the 2005 House of Lords report *Assisted Dying*, <www.
publications.parliament.uk/pa/ld/ldasdy.htm>.

Legalizing euthanasia?
1 An earlier version of this piece was published in *Search: A Church of
Ireland Journal*, vol. 32, no. 3, Autumn 2009.

Index